During the 2007-2008 Financial Crisis, several large U.S. financial institutions either faced insolvency or became insolvent as investors lost confidence in the financial system and traditional funding sources evaporated. Self-preservation efforts led many banks and broker-dealers to seek (often unsuccessfully) funding from private equity firms, competitors, and sovereign-wealth funds. Warren Buffett received several such funding requests because he had ready access to large amounts of capital and an investment from a trusted and savvy investor such as Buffett carried an imprimatur that the investment was likely to be sound.[3] But not even Mr. Buffett had sufficient resources to single-handedly recapitalize the many struggling U.S. financial firms. Nevertheless, other avenues for private funding seemed haphazard and potentially hazardous for many U.S. financial firms as they struggled to survive in a dangerous world that they helped to create but that now seemed destined to destroy them. In the absence of trusted and reliable sources of private funding, struggling firms were forced either to submit to an uncertain and unwieldy bankruptcy process or to risk being subjected to an *ad hoc* government-facilitated take-over, the terms for which were opaque and seemingly subject to change at a moment's notice. Transactions where public funding was used were sure to provoke public outrage and a painful berating by Congress. The public outcry over such taxpayer-funded rescues and the absence of more politically palatable alternatives led Congress to include provisions in the Dodd-Frank Wall Street Reform and Consumer Protection Act ("Dodd-Frank Act") that provide a framework for a government liquidation of a struggling financial firm that is not federally insured and that poses a

---

[3] Mr. Buffett only half-heartedly entertained most of these pleas for capital before finally investing in Goldman Sachs as the Crisis reached a crescendo. *See* Andrew Bary, *Barron's Insight: Warren Buffett Makes an Offer Goldman Sachs Can't Refuse*, WALL ST. J., Sept. 28, 2008, at p.3.

significant risk to the financial stability of the United States "that mitigates such risk and minimizes moral hazard."[4] Although the Dodd-Frank Act and the rules of the Federal Deposit Insurance Corporation ("FDIC") promulgated under that Act[5] codify and clarify the government's authority to take over a struggling non-bank financial firm, they may not make that alternative much more politically palatable than the *ad hoc* approaches used during the Financial Crisis. While the Dodd-Frank Act liquidation provisions are conceptually similar to those that apply to federally insured institutions, important differences could diminish the effectiveness of the former. For example, the FDIC guarantee for customer deposits of insured entities, a cornerstone of the FDIC liquidation scheme upon which the Dodd-Frank Act liquidation provisions are based, has no counterpart in the new law. As a result, customers of struggling non-insured firms would be left to fend for themselves either in proceedings of the Securities Investor Protection Corporation ("SIPC"), if applicable, or in court where they could be required to battle with competing creditors whom the new law may put on firmer footing. Without clearly defined protections for customers and would be creditors of uninsured firms, the Dodd-Frank liquidation provisions could increase the risk of a "run on the bank" type scenario for such firms if it appeared that a government liquidation of the firm was likely.

Moreover, the new law contains a number of provisions to punish current management, creditors, and shareholders. For example, the Dodd-Frank Act expressly requires that the costs of such liquidations be borne by creditors and shareholders of the distressed firm. In addition, management "responsible" for the firm's condition must be dismissed and its compensation might be clawed back. While these provisions are

---

[4] Pub. Law 111-203, 12 U.S.C. 5301 et seq.
[5] *See, e.g.*, Orderly Liquidation Authority Provisions of the Dodd-Frank Wall Street Reform and Consumer Protection Act, 76 FR 4207 (Jan. 25, 2011).

understandable from a public policy standpoint and likely were essential to gain passage of the Dodd-Frank Act, these provisions will, in practice, make the liquidation scheme highly undesirable for management, shareholders, creditors and employees of struggling firms. Therefore, creditors may be more reluctant to lend to all but the strongest firms. Management and employees of a struggling firm may be more inclined to "jump ship" at an earlier stage of a firm's decline, thereby quickening that decline. Moreover, management will be less inclined to consent to such a liquidation, and to tie up the process in court while the firm's asset waste away.

Thus, although the Dodd-Frank Act liquidation provisions might prove unworkable and punitive to struggling firms, the absence of a formalized process to facilitate the private recapitalization of struggling financial firms may leave such firms with little other alternative. Therefore, it is important to consider other alternatives to the Dodd-Frank Act approach that could minimize government involvement in a winddown of a troubled non-bank financial firm while offering incentives for private investors willing to risk capital to facilitate an efficient recapitalization.

This article discusses the difficulties that certain U.S. financial institutions faced in seeking to obtain emergency funding during the Financial Crisis and explores similarities and differences between the 2007-2008 Financial Crisis and the decline and rescue of the hedge fund, Long-Term Capital Management ("LTCM"), a decade earlier. It also analyzes the Dodd-Frank Act provisions that authorize government liquidation of non-bank financial firms and the rules promulgated and proposed by the FDIC to implement those provisions. It contends that this framework, although providing regulators with a necessary tool for liquidating struggling firms that was unavailable during the 2007-2008 Crisis, contains certain shortcomings that may make it unworkable.

4

It asserts that there may be benefits to promoting--through favorable regulatory treatment, tax incentives, or otherwise--the formation of private consortia of liquidity providers, which could include banks, broker-dealers, large institutional investors, and private equity firms with ready sources of cash that have the flexibility to provide short-term capital infusions to financial institutions in times of crisis. It concludes that a formalized structure to promote private liquidity consortia could serve as a preferable alternative to both the Dodd-Frank Act liquidation provisions and to the type of *ad hoc* consortia formed to address the failure of LTCM and, ten years later, the impending bankruptcy of Lehman Brothers.

I.   Flashback to LTCM

At the time of the Financial Crisis, the near-collapse and industry rescue of LTCM was still fresh in the collective memory of the financial community. The LTCM rescue by a consortium of private financial institutions raised many of the same issues as those involved in the 2008 crisis. Therefore, a brief discussion of LTCM and the lessons of that rescue are warranted.[6]

A.   As Global Crisis Spreads High Leverage and Illiquid Assets Drain LTCM's Capital

Prior to 1998, LTCM, which was formed in 1994,[7] had a capital base of approximately $4.8 billion.[8] LTCM built its portfolio on sophisticated arbitrage trading strategies and a significant degree of leverage thanks to favorable credit offered by

---

[6] During the LTCM crisis I worked as an attorney at the Securities and Exchange Commission ("SEC") and helped draft Congressional testimony regarding LTCM.

[7] Statement by William J. McDonough, President, Federal Reserve Bank of New York ("FRBNY") Before The Committee on Banking and Financial Services. U.S. House Of Representatives (Oct. 1, 1998) (hereinafter "McDonough Testimony").

[8] Testimony of Richard R. Lindsey, Director, SEC Division of Market Regulation Before the House Committee on Banking and Financial Services, Concerning Hedge Fund Activities in the U.S. Financial Markets (Oct. 1, 1998) (hereinafter "Lindsey Testimony").

several large banks to increase its expected returns.[9] One of the strategies LTCM employed involved shorting Treasury bond futures while taking long positions in higher yielding (and higher risk) mortgage-backed or corporate debt securities.[10] This strategy can generate profits if the difference in yields of the two types of instruments remains stable or declines. Using this and other trading strategies, LTCM produced annual returns of more than 40% in two of its first few years of operation.[11] At the beginning of 1998, however, LTCM management determined that investment opportunities were not sufficiently attractive to support adequate returns on LTCM's capital base and LTCM returned approximately $2.7 billion (or roughly one-half of its capital base) to its investors.

In the summer of 1998, as financial turmoil spread in Russia and other emerging markets, prices for high quality sovereign debt like U.S. Treasuries spiked as investors fled riskier debt instruments.[12] As the global financial crisis worsened, it became clear to LTCM that many of the assumptions in the positions it held were incorrect. LTCM's

---

[9] Statement by Patrick M. Parkinson, Associate Director, Division of Research and Statistics, Board of Governors of the Federal Reserve System, before the Committee on Agriculture, Nutrition, and Forestry, U.S. Senate (Dec. 16, 1998) ("LTCM appears to have received very generous credit terms, even though it took an exceptional degree of risk.... In LTCM's case, counterparties obtained information from LTCM that indicated that it had securities and derivatives positions that were very large relative to its capital. However, few, if any, seem to have really understood LTCM's risk profile, especially its very large positions in certain illiquid markets. Instead, they appear to have made credit decisions primarily on the basis of LTCM's past performance and the reputation of its partners.").

[10] LTCM maintained a global portfolio of debt, equity and arbitrage positions in both developed and emerging markets. *See* ROGER LOWENSTEIN, WHEN GENIUS FAILED: THE RISE AND FALL OF LONG-TERM CAPITAL MANAGEMENT 234 (2000).

[11] McDonough Testimony, *supra* note 7.

[12] On August 17, 1998, Russia effectively devalued the ruble and declared a moratorium on the payment of ruble-denominated foreign debt, which greatly increased volatility in the world's equity and debt markets. Spreads between U.S. Treasury securities and higher-yielding debt instruments widened sharply and unexpectedly. *See* McDonough Testimony, *supra* note 7. *See also Bonds Trade Narrowly, Rising on Devaluation Of the Ruble but Checked by Strong U.S. Stocks*, WALL ST. J., Aug. 18, 1998, at p. 1.

portfolio suffered losses greatly exceeding those that LTCM's models had predicted were possible, which eroded its already-depleted capital base.[13]

Recognizing LTCM's tenuous financial condition, its counterparties marked LTCM's positions to market daily and required additional collateral to compensate for the mark-to-market losses.[14] As word leaked out about LTCM's positions, some in the markets suspected that competing traders expressly targeted LTCM's portfolio to drive the fund lower and possibly make LTCM an attractive take-over target.[15] As the crisis came to a head, LTCM's capital shrank to $600 million. Potential sources of liquidity and additional capital evaporated and the firm faced insolvency.[16]

The FRBNY and the Department of Treasury determined that an abrupt and disorderly close-out of LTCM's positions would pose unacceptable risks to the U.S. economy. The perceived risks were manifold. First, had LTCM been put in default, its counterparties would have immediately closed out their positions simultaneously. The regulators concluded that LTCM's counterparties would have been unable to liquidate collateral or establish offsetting positions at previously existing prices, which would have led to sharp market moves and heavy losses for some of those counterparties. The regulators also anticipated that LTCM's counterparties' rush to close out their positions would have harmed other market participants that had no direct exposure to LTCM. Regulators believed that as anticipated losses spread to these additional market participants, credit and interest rate markets risked extreme price moves and might

---

[13] From January through August 1998, LTCM lost $2.5 billion, 52% of its $4.8 billion of equity. Most of those losses occurred in August. As of August 31, 1998, LTCM's capital base was a mere $2.3 billion. This diminished capital base supported recorded trading positions totaling $107 billion, yielding a leverage ratio in excess of 50-to-1. At one point LTCM was a party to 7,000 derivative contracts with a notional value of $1.4 trillion. LOWENSTEIN, *supra* note 10, at 179-180.

[14] Marking to market means assigning a value to a position held in a financial instrument based on the current fair market price for the instrument or similar instruments.

[15] *See* LOWENSTEIN, *supra* note 10, at 172-73.

[16] Lindsey Testimony, *supra* note 8.

temporarily cease to function. The regulators concluded that a disorderly wind-down of LTCM ultimately could increase the cost of capital to U.S. businesses.[17]

B. Regulators Host a Consortium Of Financial Firms To Address LTCM's Imminent Failure

The regulators determined that "the responsible public policy objective was to get together those with a direct financial interest in an orderly rescue of Long-Term Capital, to discuss its problems openly and objectively, to provide a sounding board for solutions, and if necessary, a calming influence."[18]

On September 22, 1998, the FRBNY hosted Goldman Sachs, Merrill Lynch, and JP Morgan, which had the greatest knowledge of the LTCM's plight. The firms discussed various approaches to stabilizing LTCM, including the concept of a "collective industry" or consortium approach. They all agreed, however, that if any firm or group of firms wished to step forward and buy LTCM itself or buy LTCM's positions this outcome would be the most desirable. In the absence of other solutions, however, the firms studied the possibility of "lifting" the equity and fixed income positions out of LTCM, or, in the alternative, the formation of a consortium to take over the entire firm.[19] The firms determined that lifting LTCM's positions would not be feasible but that an industry consortium take-over might be. Nevertheless, such an approach was still viewed as a "last ditch" effort.

At this point, the firms learned that an "investor group" was prepared to make an offer for LTCM. The investor group, which Goldman Sachs had reportedly lined up, was

---

[17] McDonough Testimony, *supra* note 7.

[18] *Id.*

[19] The firms included UBS, a Swiss bank that had a large stake in LTCM. *Fallout From Long-Term Capital's Near Failure Spreads Across the European Banking Sector*, WALL ST. J., Sept. 28, 1998, at p.1. The number of firms was eventually expanded to thirteen.

headed by none other than Warren Buffett.[20] The Goldman/Buffett investor group

reportedly would have forced the resignation of LTCM's founder, John Meriwether, and

may have, over time, been less financially generous to the original LTCM owners.[21]

LTCM failed to accept Buffett's short-fused bid, reportedly because of "legal

complications."[22]

With no other offer on the table, the consortium of firms agreed to recapitalize

LTCM. Fourteen banks and securities firms agreed to participate in the recapitalization

plan, with three firms contributing smaller amounts than the others.[23] The total

contribution was $3.65 billion for 90 percent of the equity in the fund.[24] LTCM's

---

[20] *To the Rescue? A Hedge Fund Falters, So the Fed Persuades Big Banks to Ante Up--Firms to Lend $3.6 Billion As Long-Term Capital Loses on Its Bond Bets 'Star Power' and Red Ink*, WALL ST. J., Sept. 24, 1998, at A1. LTCM reportedly sought capital from Buffett on multiple occasions prior to his being contacted by Goldman Sachs. LTCM also unsuccessfully sought funding from Soros Fund Management, Merrill Lynch, PaineWebber (now part of UBS), Tiger Management, Ziff Brothers, and LTCM's own investors. *All Bets Are Off: How the Salesmanship and Brainpower Failed at Long-Term Capital—Investors Clamored to Get In, While Partners Debated Their Ever-Greater Risks—On the Payroll, 25 Ph.D.s.* WALL ST. J., Nov. 16, 1998, at A1 (hereinafter "All Bets Are Off").

[21] *Greenspan Defends Long-Term Capital Plan --- More Threats Lurk in Market, Fed Chairman Testifies; Lawmakers Are Critical*, WALL ST. J., Oct. 2, 1998, at p.1. Buffett reportedly told Goldman that "[t]he only way I'll do this is if we jointly buy the portfolio and you [Goldman] take over the portfolio company." *All Bets Are Off, supra* note. In addition to Buffett, who was prepared to invest at least $3 billion in LTCM, Goldman itself was prepared to invest $300 million and committed to enlist AIG to contribute $700 million for a total capital infusion of $4 billion.

[22] Meriwether purportedly did not accept Buffett's bid before it expired because he could not get the approval of his partners to accept the bid on such short notice. *All Bets Are Off, supra* note 20. *See also How Buffett, AIG and Goldman Sought Long-Term Capital, but Were Rejected*, WALL ST. J., Sept. 30, 1998, at C1. It also has been suggested that the Goldman/Buffett bid, which totaled five paragraphs, had an hour-long deadline, and exhibited a clear misunderstanding of the complexity of LTCM's partnership structure, may have been too simple and arbitrary. After signing off on the bid, Buffett was "bizarrely unreachable" until after the bid was withdrawn. LOWENSTEIN, *supra* note 10, at 203-205.

[23] McDonough Testimony, *supra* note 7. For example, Lehman Brothers, which itself was facing financial difficulties, contributed only $100 million. *All Bets Are Off, supra* note 20. Other contributors included: Bankers Trust Corporation; Barclays PLC; Chase Manhattan Corp.; Credit Suisse First Boston Company; Deutsche Bank AG; Goldman Sachs Group LP; J.P. Morgan & Co.; Merrill Lynch & Co. Inc.; Morgan Stanley Dean Witter & Co.; Paribas; Salomon Smith Barney (Traveler Group); Société Generale; and UBS AG. *Long-Term Capital Management: Regulators Need to Focus Greater Attention on Systemic Risk*, GAO, Oct. 1999 at n.7 (hereinafter "LTCM GAO Report"). Paribas and Société Generale were only willing to contribute $125 million each, while the others contributed $300 million each. *See* LOWENSTEIN, supra note 10, at 207.

[24] *LTCM GAO Report, supra* note at n.7. *See also* LOWENSTEIN, *supra* note 10, at 207-208.

existing partners would receive the remaining 10 percent, valued at $400 million.[25] The

banks agreed to a three-part agenda: (1) reduce the fund's risk exposure; (2) return capital

to new investors; and, if possible, (3) realize a profit.[26] Although the consortium

considered removing LTCM's management, it realized that given the size and complexity

of LTCM's positions doing so could compromise their efforts to quickly and efficient

unwind LTCM's portfolio. Ultimately, to ensure that LTCM management did not bolt to

start a new fund the consortium agreed to pay them bonuses for managing the portfolio.[27]

Bear, LTCM's clearing firm, declined to contribute to the rescue, noting that Bear

Stearn's clearing risk to LTCM was "a helluva lot more than $250 to $300 million," the

amount that the consortium members were being encouraged to contribute.[28] The

decision not to participate in the consortium raised suspicion among some consortium

members that Bear knew something that they did not.[29] Although consortium members

were assured that Bear Stearn's decision was not motivated by unique information about

LTCM's financial condition its decision not to participate was a lingering source of

resentment among consortium members.

No public funds were spent or committed on the LTCM recapitalization.[30]

---

[25] LOWENSTEIN. *supra* note 10, at 208.

[26] *Id.* at 207.

[27] *Id.* at 216.

[28] Clearing firms for large and complex hedge funds are often referred to as prime brokers. In addition to execution and clearance of transactions, prime brokers also provide margin financing, centralized custody. securities lending, and administrative services such as risk reporting. Senior Supervisors Group. Risk Management Lessons from the Global Banking Crisis of 2008, Oct. 21, 2009, at 32. As LTCM's prime broker. it could be argued that Bear was in the best position to determine the consolidated risk that LTCM had assumed and to take the necessary steps to require LTCM to limit LTCM's exposure to Bear and to the markets generally. Indeed, even before LTCM began to raise concerns for the broader market. Bear was anxious about the amount of capital it was risking with LTCM. Unlike many other Wall Street firms, Bear generally required LTCM to take "hair cuts" on the securities it used to collateralize its financing with Bear and agreed to keep clearing for LTCM only if the hedge fund maintained $1.5 billion at Bear. *See* LOWENSTEIN. supra note 10, at 85-86. Moreover. Bear was holding $500 million in collateral from LTCM. *Id.* at 205.

[29] *All Bets Are Off, supra* note 20.

[30] McDonough Testimony, *supra* note 7.

Subsequent to the rescue of LTCM the consortium oversaw all trading by the firm and had the authority to veto decisions made by LTCM's partners. Although the firm continued to register losses immediately after the bailout, as the market rebounded LTCM began to recover before its holdings were liquidated.[31]

After the rescue, many were critical of the government's role in facilitating the rescue. Indeed, at a subsequent hearing, Congressman Jim Leach asserted that Meriwether may have rejected the Goldman/Buffett-led offer knowing that the FRB was worried enough about the fallout to ensure that LTCM was rescued.[32] Nevertheless, the government also won some praise for its role.[33]

C.   Takeaways From LTCM Crisis

The LTCM rescue framed a number of issues that would be amplified in the broader crisis a decade later. Therefore, it is useful to highlight a few details of the LTCM matter to compare and contrast it with the tumult to come.

1. Consortium Was Effective But May Have Undermined Alternatives: The

consortium accomplished two important goals: (1) it limited what could

potentially have been a much more severe market crisis by neutralizing LTCM as

---

[31] *All Bets Are Off, supra* note 20 and *As Markets Swing, Meriwether Hears Echoes of His Own Collapse; LTCM Lost Billions a Decade Ago; Now A Second Fall*, WALL ST. J., Sept. 20, 2008, at B1 (detailing the struggles of JWM Partners LLC, another Meriwether-managed fund which Meriwether subsequently liquidated). *See also Meriwether is Shutting Hedge Fund, Sans Drama*, WALL ST. J., July 9, 2009, at C1 and LOWENSTEIN. *supra* note 10, at 229 ("Though Wall Street recovered, Long-Term's brand of arbitrage did not. Under its new owners, the fund enjoyed a good last quarter in 1998 and a good start to the new year; then it went into a tailspin....In the first year after the bailout the fund earned 10 percent....[T]he fund redeemed the consortium's $3.65 billion in capital. For practical purposes. the fund had liquidated by early 2000.").

[32] *All Bets Are Off, supra* note 20. *Compare* Craig Furfine. *The Costs and Benefits of Moral Suasion: Evidence from the Rescue of Long-Term Capital Management*, Journal of Business. vol. 79, no.2 (2006) (banks involved in the LTCM rescue borrowed less unsecured funds after the rescue than before and paid higher rates than comparable banks that were not involved in the rescue, which could discount a "Too Big Too Fail" effect caused by the FRB's involvement).

[33] *See, e.g., Bailout Allows Japanese to Lecture U.S. Tokyo's Call for Tougher Controls Has Familiar Ring*. WALL ST. J., Sept. 28, 1998, at p.1 (U.S. earns praise for preventing LTCM crisis from spreading to the broader market amidst accusation of hypocrisy for criticizing Japanese "convoy system" of prodding stronger financial institutions to mask problems of the weak while encouraging that approach with LTCM).

a potential catalyst for a broader crisis; and (2) it liquidated LTCM's positions in an orderly manner, thereby preventing a "fire sale" of those assets and related asset classes. It accomplished these two goals by taking over all assets and liabilities of LTCM and used only private financing. The consortium had the authority to dismiss current management but to promote continuity retained key LTCM managers and staff. By providing a government-facilitated alternative, however, the consortium may have emboldened LTCM's management not to accept the bid from the Goldman/Buffett-led investment group, which was less favorable to LTCM's management although not necessarily so to LTCM's shareholders. Under this rationale, the consortium effectively established a floor value for LTCM, potentially emboldening management of distressed firms in the future to wait for government intervention before agreeing to a private take-over. As a practical matter, however, the Goldman/Buffett bid appeared to be little more than an expression of interest, which neither Buffett nor Goldman appeared to be fully behind.[34] Nevertheless, it is difficult gauge what effect, if any, the presence of the consortium had on the Goldman/Buffett bid. And while it is possible that the Government's involvement in organizing the LTCM rescue could have discouraged future private liquidity providers from bidding on troubled firms in the future, such effect, if any, would be difficult if not impossible to quantify. It is important to distinguish this issue from the related issue of whether LTCM's creditors were more likely to loan to LTCM because

---

[34] It is difficult to fault LTCM for not jumping at the Goldman/Buffett bid given that Buffett had, prior to the bid, repeatedly said he was not interested in investing in LTCM and the bid was little more than a few paragraphs of deal points on a one-page fax that mischaracterized the partnership structure of LTCM and allowed no opportunity for amendment or clarification. Never mind the fact that LTCM (and others) suspected that Goldman traders had downloaded LTCM's positions and were using the information to trade against them. *See* LOWENSTEIN, *supra* note 10, at 181, 202-204.

they assumed that if the firm got into trouble the Government would lead the charge to bail them out. Some commenters at the time viewed the Government's involvement in the rescue as the "camel's nose under the tent" with respect to extending the "too big to fail" doctrine to non-regulated hedge funds.[35] The FRB did not dispute that Government involvement may have created some moral hazard.[36]

2. **Capital Required Was Modest**: Although LTCM was able to accumulate trading positions in excess of $100 billion, the rescue package, which effectively staved off a broader market crisis, was only $3.6 billion. Presumably, the structure of the deal, the contributors, and the role of the U.S. Government—and not the size of the rescue package alone--sent a strong message to the markets that decisive action would be taken to prevent LTCM's fall from spreading to the broader market.[37]

3. **Major Counterparties Were Relatively Stable**: Although LTCM was on the verge of bankruptcy when the consortium formed, those most likely to suffer as a result of LTCM's failure (*i.e.*, the consortium members and LTCM's clearing firm) were financially stable. Even Lehman, whose own viability was rumored to

---

[35] *See* LOWENSTEIN, *supra* note 9. at 208.

[36] *Id.* at 229-230.

[37] The Goldman/Buffett-led group estimated the cost of an LTCM recapitalization to be $4 billion. The similarity of the two valuations may suggest that both the Goldman/Buffett group and the consortium were planning to wind down LTCM and the only difference in the valuations was reflected by the fact that Goldman/Buffett was proposing to buy 95% of LTCM (for a total firm valuation of $4.21 billion) while not retaining management whereas the consortium was bidding for 90% of LTCM (for a total valuation of $4 billion) and intended to supervise current management in the wind down. Goldman's involvement in both groups may bring into question the independence of the two valuations. Interestingly. Goldman's financial contribution would be the same to either effort--$300 million. In hindsight, Buffett's involvement in the LTCM matter may have been exaggerated. Other than a tepid, hour-long commitment to help bankroll Goldman's liquidation of LTCM's positions. Buffett seems not to have made a meaningful contribution to the process, other than perhaps fodder for the critics of the FRB's involvement in the process. I found no convincing evidence that the FRB's involvement in coordinating the rescue discouraged any alternative recapitalization efforts. And in fairness to Uncle Warren, Wall Street called him, he didn't call them.

be at issue during the market crisis that led to LTCM's demise, was able to

contribute $100 million to the consortium. Bear's unwillingness to contribute

appears not to have been motivated by an inability to contribute but rather by a

belief, obviously not shared by consortium members, that its role as LTCM's

clearing broker was sacrifice enough. To be sure, several consortium members

suffered staggering losses after the rescue, but the losses were not fatal.[38]

4. **U.S. Government Role Was Limited But Instrumental**: Notwithstanding that

no U.S. Government funds were used in or committed to the LTCM bail-out, the

importance of the Government's role in facilitating the bail-out cannot be

overstated. Although participation in the consortium was not legally compelled,

the FRBNY brought the group together to do a deal and undoubtedly member

firms would be held accountable if they failed to reach an agreement.[39]

II. Fast-forward to 2007: The Calamity Begins

A. Bear Stearns' High Grade Funds Collapse[40]

The summer of 2007 marked a watershed in the credit crisis and in hindsight may

have signaled the end of an era for the U.S. investment banking industry. In June 2007,

two hedge funds operated by Bear edged toward insolvency. The two funds (High Grade

---

[38] LOWENSTEIN. *supra* note 10, at 221-222.

[39] *See, e.g., id.* at 230 ("[T]he banks would not have come together without the enormous power and influence of the Fed behind them. and without a joint effort. Long-Term surely would have collapsed.").

[40] Bear operated under a holding company structure. The Bear Companies Inc., the holding company, operated principally through its broker-dealer and international bank subsidiaries, which included Bear, Stearns & Co. Inc.. Bear Securities Corp.. Bear International Limited. and Bear Bank plc. The Company was regulated by the SEC as a consolidated supervised entity ("CSE"), under which it was subject to group-wide supervision and examination by the SEC. Provided that Bear held tentative net capital in excess of $1 billion and net capital in excess of $500 million. Bear was permitted to calculate its net capital charges for market risk and derivatives-related credit risk based on mathematical models. At May 31, 2007, Bear had net capital of $3.17 billion, far in excess of the minimum required to qualify for the CSE program. Bear's gross leverage (*i.e.*, total assets divided by stockholders' equity including preferred and trust preferred equity) at the time was 31.2 and had total assets of $423.3 billion. *Bear 10-Q for the quarterly period ended May 31, 2007.*

Structured Credit Strategies Fund and the more highly leveraged High Grade Structured

Credit Strategies Enhanced Leverage Fund) invested in complex securities comprised of

bonds backed by subprime mortgages.[41] The funds used leverage to enhance returns.

But as the value of the securities in which the funds invested plummeted, their use of

leverage exacerbated the losses the funds suffered.[42] As the funds neared insolvency,

firms that lent to the funds threatened to seize and liquidate collateral that the funds had

used to secure the loans.[43] Under pressure from the funds' lenders, Bear reluctantly

provided a $3.2 billion credit line to one of the funds in an attempt to stabilize it. The

credit line increased Bear's own financial exposure to the funds, which had originally

been only $40 million.[44] The move marked the largest bail-out of a hedge fund since

LTCM.[45] By mid-July 2007, the net value of assets in the most highly leveraged of the

two Bear funds was zero and that of the other fund was 9% of what it was in March 2007.

In late July, Bear proceeded to unwind both funds.[46] The collapse of the two funds,

which at one point managed $20 billion in assets, reportedly cost investors more than $1

---

[41] Kate Kelly et al. *Two Big Funds at Bear Face Shutdown; As Rescue Plan Falters Amid Subprime Woes, Merrill Asserts Claims*, WALL ST. J.. June 20. 2007. at A1.

[42] The two Bear funds invested in illiquid securities (*i.e.*, they are not actively traded) backed by subprime mortgages (home loans extended to borrowers with poor credit histories). The funds used these securities as collateral for the loans the funds used to finance its operations. Because the securities are not actively traded, they are difficult to value, and often are valued with pricing models. Such models can vary widely by firm, however. The crisis was brought to a head when firms that lent to the funds threatened to seize the collateral and sell it to satisfy the loans. The threat of large amounts of illiquid securities dumped onto the market put extreme downward pressure on the prices of those securities. *See Kelly, supra* note.

[43] *$3.2 Billion Move By Bear to Rescue Fund*. N.Y. Times. June 23, 2007, at A1 (hereinafter "$3.2 Billion Move"); *Bear Staves Off Collapse of 2 Hedge Funds*. N.Y. Times. June 21. 2007, at C1 (while JP Morgan, Goldman Sachs, and Bank of America reached agreements with Bear to preclude collateral liquidations, Merrill Lynch proceeded to auction the collateral it had seized and Deutsche Bank appeared to do so as well). Bear took flack for its initial reluctance to bail out the funds, contending that the money in the funds belonged to large institutions, wealthy individuals and lenders who knew the risks before they invested. *See The Fall of Bear: Lost Opportunities Haunt Final Days of Bear; Executives Bickered Over Raising Cash, Cutting Mortgages*. WALL ST. J., May 27, 2008. at A1 (hereinafter "The Fall of Bear Part 1 of 3"). This article was the first of three regarding the fall of Bear that appeared in the *Wall Street Journal* from May 27. 2008, to May 29, 2008.

[44] *Lifeline: Bear Bails Out Fund With Big Loan; Injection of $3.2 Billion Caps Days of Drama; Subprime Sector Fears*, WALL ST. J., June 23, 2007, at A1.

[45] *$3.2 Billion Move, supra* note 43.

[46] *Bear Seizes Most of Fund's Collateral*, WALL ST. J., July 27, 2007, at C5.

billion and worsened a developing credit crisis.[47] The collapse also damaged Bear's

reputation as a prudent risk manager. An August 2007 investor conference call intended

to calm investors and the ouster of the high-level Bear executive who oversaw the failed

hedge funds only made matters worse.[48]

By March 2008, as the credit crisis worsened, confidence in Bear faded.[49] On

March 10, 2008, a bundle of home loans that Bear had packaged and sold received a poor

credit rating from a large rating agency. The downgrade triggered rumors about Bear's

financial condition.[50] On March 11, 2008, the FRB launched a huge credit facility to

---

[47] *Fed Races to Rescue Bear in Bid to Steady Financial System; Storied Firm Sees Stock Price Plunge 47%; J.P. Morgan Steps In*, WALL ST. J., March 15, 2008, at A1 (hereinafter "Fed Races to Rescue Bear"). *See also Wall Street, Bear Hit Again By Investors Fleeing Mortgage Sector*, WALL ST. J., Aug. 1, 2007, at A1 (Bear prevents investors from withdrawing money from another Bear-operated fund). *U.S. Stocks Plunge On Higher Yields, Mortgage Bond Concern*, Bloomberg, June 20, 2007 (Merrill Lynch seizes collateral from funds run by Bear, which recently controlled more than $20 billion and had $9 billion in loans).

[48] *The Fall of Bear, Part 1 of 3, supra* note 43. Responding to what it saw as an opportunity to buy a piece of Bear at an attractive price, leveraged buyout firm Kohlberg Kravis Roberts & Co. ("KKR") made an overture to Bear but no deal materialized, due in part to Bear's concern that a deal with KKR might offend Bear clients that competed with KKR. *Id.* Section 619(a)(1) of the Dodd-Frank Act, with important limitations, restricts a "banking entity" from engaging in proprietary trading or acquiring or retaining any equity, partnership, or other ownership interest in, or sponsoring a hedge fund or a private equity fund. These provisions are referred to as the "Volcker Rule," after former Fed. Chairman Paul Volcker, who advocated the limitations. Section 619(a)(2) of the Dodd-Frank Act, which applies to nonbank financial companies supervised by the Fed. imposes additional capital requirements for and additional quantitative limits regarding proprietary trading or taking an equity or other interest in a hedge fund or private equity fund. Although the hedge fund provisions of the Volcker Rule appear designed to address the type of arrangements between Bear Stearns and its affiliates hedge funds Bear Stearns would not likely have met the definition of "banking entity" in Section 619(h)(1) of the Act and therefore would not have been prohibited from owning affiliated hedge funds. 12 U.S.C. 1851(h)(1). Moreover, in light of a number of exceptions to the general hedge fund ownership provisions, it is not clear to what extent, if any, Section 619 of the Dodd-Frank Act would have restricted Bear Stearns' ownership of the affiliated funds. On the other hand, in the future, the Volcker Rule could restrict or at least complicate banks from entering into the types of arrangements that resulted in the LTCM rescue.

[49] *Fed Races to Rescue Bear, supra* note 47.

[50] *Ratings Downgrades Spur Action in Bear Puts*, WALL ST. J., March 11, 2008, at C7. To understand the liquidity crunch that Bear faced at this point it is important to understand the way in which Bear, like many other financial firms, funded its operations. Bear's short-term cash sources consisted principally of collateralized borrowings, including repos, sell/buy arrangements, securities lending arrangements, and customer short balances. Bear viewed these sources as more stable than short-term unsecured borrowings, which subjected the firm to "roll-over" risk because the providers of credit are not obligated to refinance the instruments at maturity. Repos also enjoy special treatment under the U.S. Bankruptcy Code (*i.e.*, they can't be clawed back by the trustee after a filing), which, some have argued, could have sped Bear's demise. *See* Thomas Jackson and David A. Skeel, "Transaction Consistency and the New Finance In Bankruptcy," Scholarship at Penn Law, Paper 355 (2011) 11-12. Short-term unsecured funding sources

allow investment banks to obtain loans from the Government collateralized by a much broader array of assets, including mortgage securities, than had previously been the case.[51] On the heals of the news of the downgrade and the new credit facility Bear's stock price plummeted, falling to $57 from $172 in January of 2007.[52] Some large investment banks stopped accepting trades that would expose them to Bear and some money funds reduced their holdings of short-term debt that Bear issued.[53] Hedge funds that used Bear to clear their trades and to provide financing drained cash from their accounts with Bear.[54] Securities firms that had been willing to accept collateral from Bear now demanded cash.[55] As Bear's cash position shriveled, the firm contacted JP

---

included commercial paper, medium-term notes and bank borrowings, which typically had maturities ranging from overnight to one year. To manage roll-over risk Bear maintained a liquidity pool. Bear also used equity and long-term debt as longer-term sources of unsecured financing. Bear also attested to an alternative funding strategy, which was intended to enable the firm to weather an "event-driven liquidity crisis." The alternative funding strategy was designed to allow Bear to maintain sufficient "cash capital" (i.e., equity plus long-term debt maturing in more than 12 months) and funding sources to enable Bear to refinance short-term, unsecured borrowings with fully secured borrowings. The 12-month time frame assumed that Bear would not or could not liquidate assets and could not issue unsecured debt, including commercial paper. Bear maintained collateral for secured borrowing in various subsidiaries, both regulated and unregulated. not in the parent. It noted the potential that regulators might prevent the flow of funds or securities from a regulated subsidiary to the parent or to an unregulated subsidiary. In recognition of the potential that collateral might be "trapped" within a regulated subsidiary, the parent company maintained a minimum of $5.0 billion of immediately accessible liquidity. This so-called "Parent Company Liquidity Pool" measured $11.3 billion at the end of June 2007. Its "net cash capital," (i.e., cash capital in excess of that portion of assets that cannot be funded on a secured basis) was $2.3 billion. but averaged just $913 million over the previous seven months of fiscal year 2007. well below the firm's own target of $2 billion. The company also maintained various committed credit facilities that would allow the parent and certain subsidiaries to borrow on a secured or unsecured based, depending on the facility. The facilities typically had covenants that required the maintenance of a certain level of stockholder's equity. *Bear 10Q.*

[51] *Stocks Surge As Fed Offers a Boost.* Wash. Post, March 12. 2008, at A1.

[52] KATE KELLY, STREET FIGHTERS: THE LAST 72 HOURS OF BEAR, THE TOUGHEST FIRM ON WALL STREET 9, 13 & 113 (2009).

[53] Statement By Timothy F. Geithner, President and Chief Executive Officer. FRBNY, before the U.S. Senate Committee on Banking, Housing and Urban Affairs Regarding Actions by the FRBNY in Response to Liquidity Pressures in Financial Markets (Apr. 3. 2008) 9.

[54] *Fed Races to Rescue Bear, supra* note 47. In one week hedge funds and other prime-brokerage customers had withdrawn $13.9 billion from Bear, leaving the firm with only about $3 billion in cash. KELLY, *supra* note 52. at 45-46. In early March 2008. the cost of credit default swaps, insurance against the possibility of Bear defaulting on its debt, spiked as did so-called "novation requests," requests by investors (e.g., hedge funds) to be bought out of securities contracts they had entered into with Bear. *The Fall of Bear: Fear, Rumors Touched Off Fatal Run on Bear; Executives Swung from Hope to Despair in the Space of a Week,* WALL ST. J., May 28, 2008, at A1 (hereinafter "The Fall of Bear, Part 2 of 3").

[55] Bear's primary regulator, the SEC, stated that neither the regulatory program under which Bear was subject nor the Basel Committee on Banking Supervision (Basel II), which develops international capital

17

Morgan, its clearing bank, to seek a $25 billion line of credit.[56] JP Morgan agreed to

consider making the loan and began assembling a team to explore it.

Bear also retained investment bank Lazard to explore a "gamut" of alternatives

for saving the firm.[57] Bear also retained a bankruptcy attorney to begin exploring the

possibility of a bankruptcy filing. With nearly five hundred subsidiaries, such a filing

promised to be a monumental task.[58]

Lazard contacted potential investors that it thought might have an interest in

lending to or taking an equity stake in Bear. One such prospective investor was

Christopher Flowers, the billionaire founder of J.C. Flowers & Co., a private investment

---

standards for banks, considered the possibility that secured financing (*e.g.*, repos) that was backed by high-quality collateral could become completely unavailable. *SEC Office of Inspector General, Semiannual Report to Congress*, April 1, 2008 – September 30, 2008 at 21-22. And yet for Bear it had. The day the SEC Inspector General's Report was released then-SEC Chairman Christopher Cox announced that the SEC was ending the CSE program. In doing so he stated "[t]he last six months have made it abundantly clear that voluntary regulation does not work. When Congress passed the Gramm-Leach-Bliley Act [of 1999. Pub. L. 106-102. 113 Stat. 1338, which repealed provisions of the Glass-Steagall Act of 1933 that had restricted commercial banks, investment banks, and insurance companies from combining within a single entity], it created a significant regulatory gap by failing to give to the SEC or any agency the authority to regulate large investment bank holding companies, like Goldman Sachs, Morgan Stanley, Merrill Lynch, Lehman Brothers, and Bear." SEC Press Release 2008-230 (Sept. 26, 2008). *See also* Report of Anton R. Valukas. Examiner. March 11, 2010, at nn. 5733-34 and accompanying text (neither the SEC nor any other agency was given statutory authority to regulate systemically important large investment bank holding companies, a gap which the SEC intended to fill in 2004 with the creation of the CSE program). Although the CSE program was technically voluntary, a firm that withdrew from the program would be subject to regulation by the European Union, which major investment banks viewed as less preferable. *Id.* at nn. 5732 & 5735-36 and accompanying text. Some firms appear to have been better prepared for weathering the credit crisis than others. *See* Payments Risk Committee Report of the Task Force on Tri-Party Repo Infrastructure (May 17, 2010) at 4 ("Some Dealers did not properly anticipate the potential for secured financing to be unavailable, even for high quality collateral. Some Dealers became excessively reliant on short-term repo financing, especially in regard to collateral types that were or became illiquid and subject to valuation uncertainty, contributing to greater leverage in the system.").

[56] KELLY. *supra* note 52, at 42. It is unclear whether Bear ever tapped any of its committed credit facilities. *See supra* note 50. While awaiting a response from JP Morgan, Bear executives also considered approaching Warren Buffett for financing. *Id.* at 43. Bear also considered a deal with Citadel Investment Group, but eventually rejected pursuing that avenue because Bear believed that Citadel might not have the resources to complete such a large deal and Bear was reluctant to allow Citadel to look at Bear's books for fear that Citadel would use the information to bet against Bear. *Id.* at 130.

[57] *See Fed Races to Rescue Bear, supra* note 47.

[58] KELLY, *supra* note 52, at 43-45.

firm that specializes in financial industry acquisitions.[59] Mr. Flowers had approached

Bear the previous fall about a possible investment, but Bear rejected the overture,

suspicious of Flowers' intentions.[60] Lazard found Flowers an attractive suitor for Bear

for two reasons: (1) Flowers could put a deal together quickly and (2) the imprimatur of a

respected private investor might instill confidence in Bear's lenders and clients.[61] As

Bear's clearing bank and trading counterparty, JP Morgan had multiple interests in

propping up Bear, which could color any investment that the bank might make. On the

other hand, Flowers' motives might be viewed more as a reflection of Flowers'

confidence in Bear's future business prospects. Lazard opined that Bear would likely

need between $3 billion and $5 billion to restore confidence in the firm. Lazard alerted

Flowers that JP Morgan was another potential investor.[62] Flowers contacted JP Morgan

---

[59] *See* KELLY, *supra* note 52, at 40. In 2006, *Forbes* named Mr. Flowers, a former Goldman Sachs partner, one of the Top 400 richest Americans. Mr. Flowers' firm invested in financial firms that included the failed Long-Term Credit Bank of Japan, which Flowers and a consortium that included Ripplewood Holdings bought from the Japanese government in 2000 and renamed Shinsei Bank. *Forbes* (Sept. 21, 2006). [Note to self: avoid investing in firms with names beginning in "Long-Term."] Shinsei, the first Japanese bank bought by foreigners, was criticized by Japanese regulators for its reluctance to lend to risky borrowers. *Shinsei Bank Pressured to Keep Shaky Loans --- Regulators' Moves Raise Questions on Japanese Overhaul*, WALL ST. J., Sept. 26, 2001, at C1 (Ironically, the article notes that "[t]he back-and-forth between Shinsei and the [Japanese regulators] underscores the gap between regulation in Japan and countries such as the U.S. and the United Kingdom, where authorities rarely manage the setting of a bank's lending policies."). *See supra* note 33. *But see Loss At Shinsei Bank $1 Billion-Plus*, WALL ST. J., April 15, 2010, at C2 (Shinsei suffered net losses after the financial crisis due to investments in U.S. mortgage sector and domestic real estate financing). Although a frequent adviser during the financial crisis, more recently Mr. Flower's investment decisions have drawn negative scrutiny. *See, e.g., Checkmate for a Wall Street Wizard?*, Fortune, Aug. 31, 2009.

[60] KELLY, *supra* note 52, at 41. Instead, Bear's management pursued what they believed was a much more attractive option, a joint venture with the Chinese investment bank, Citic Securities Co., which would make an immediate investment of $1 billion in Bear in exchange for a similar amount to be invested by Bear in the Chinese firm over time. In addition to the immediate cash infusion, Bear was confident that the deal would enhance Bear's presence in Asia. The announcement of the deal with the Chinese in October of 2007 did little to restore confidence in Bear. Nevertheless, so confident was Bear management in the merits of the Citic deal that in early 2008 it nixed two other potential deals with the Japanese—one with Sumitomo, the other with Nomura Holdings, Inc. Bear also rejected overtures from Fortress Investment Group. *Id.* at 111-112. Additional deals between Bear and Allianz SE's Pacific Investment Management Co. failed to materialize. *The Fall of Bear, Part 1 of 3, supra* note 43. Chinese regulatory approval of the Citic deal was slow and Citic itself backed out after the JP Morgan buy-out was announced. *Citic Ditches Tie-Up Plans After Bear Deal*, WALL ST. J., March 19, 2008, at C2.

[61] KELLY, *supra* note 52, at 41.

[62] *Id.*

to determine whether they would be competing with the much larger firm in acquiring Bear. JP Morgan was noncommittal, which encouraged Flowers to forge ahead.[63]

After speaking to Bear about its need for emergency funding, JP Morgan notified the FRB of Bear's request. Separately, the SEC and Bear also notified the FRB that Bear had lost far more of its liquidity than Bear had originally believed.[64] The SEC and Bear told the FRB that Bear was nearly bankrupt.[65]

From March 13-14, 2008, the FRB, the Treasury Department and the SEC discussed possible approaches to obtain a short-term cash infusion for Bear to allow more time for an industry solution to the problem. One alternative that they considered hours before the market opened on Friday, March 14, 2008, was to bring together other securities firms which could contribute to a fund to allow Bear to open that morning. This alternative was rejected because the regulators understood that other firms were in self-preservation mode and that such an *ad hoc* arrangement could not be put together under such a short time frame.[66]

B. FRB Throws Bear A Life Line through JP Morgan

The regulators concluded that allowing Bear to fail was too risky in light of the broader market turmoil.[67] Regulators were particularly concerned about the impact that a Bear bankruptcy would have on the tri-party repo market, a $2 trillion market through which investment banks obtain short-term funding from institutional investors and others

---

[63] *Id.* at 42.

[64] *See Fed Races to Rescue Bears Stearns, supra* note 47. *See also Statement of Timothy F. Geithner, supra* note 53, at 9 ("rumors of Bear's failing financial health caused its balance of unencumbered liquidity on March 13[, 2008] to decline sharply to levels that were not adequate to cover maturing obligations and funds that could be withdrawn freely."). *See also The Fall of Bear, Part 2 of 3. supra* note 54 ("[l]enders such as Fidelity Investments were refusing to replenish the financing Bear needed to open the next morning.").

[65] *Statement of Timothy F. Geithner, supra* note 53, at 1.

[66] KELLY, *supra* note 52, at 67-68.

[67] *Statement of Timothy F. Geithner, supra* note 53, at 9-10.

with large cash reserves.[68] Therefore, the FRB arranged for a loan to Bear that would be

extended through JP Morgan, Bear Stearn's clearing bank for repo transactions.[69] The

duration of the loan was for 28 days. The amount was limited only by the amount of

collateral Bear could provide. The FRB, not JP Morgan, would bear the risk of

[68] KELLY, *supra* note 52, at 66. A brief discussion of the size, complexity, and global scope of the tri-party repo market may help illustrate why regulators were uniquely concerned about this market as Bear teetered on the brink of bankruptcy. Although economically similar to a secured loan, a repurchase agreement or "repo," is technically a sale of securities coupled with an agreement to repurchase the securities at a later date at a specified price slightly higher than the original purchase price. *See Tri-Party Repo Infrastructure Reform: A White Paper Prepared by The Federal Reserve Bank of New York* (May 17, 2010) at 5 (hereinafter "FRBNY Repo White Paper"). The tri-party repo market provides a means for certain types of firms with abundant cash reserves (*e.g.*, money market mutual funds, large banks, and corporate treasurers) to loan it, for short periods of time, to large securities firms and securities affiliates of banks, which use the cash to finance their securities inventories. The tri-party label refers to the fact that the transaction between the cash "lender" and "borrower" settles through one of two clearing banks: Bank of New York Mellon or J.P. Morgan Chase. Tri-party repos are collateralized primarily by U.S. Treasuries and mortgage-backed securities and debentures issued by Fannie Mae, Federal Home Loan Mortgage Corporation, or the Government National Mortgage Association, but other asset classes, such as corporate and municipal bonds and equity securities on deposit at the Depository Trust & Clearing Corporation ("DTCC") are also used. *Id.* at 8 and notes 6 & 7. Clearing bank collateral management systems enable dealers to use their assets maintained throughout the world to collateralize their repo transactions. *See* Letter from Gerald L. Hassell, President, Bank of New York ("BNY"), to Jennifer J. Johnson, Secretary, Federal Reserve Board (FRB Docket No. R-1122) and Jonathan G. Katz, Secretary, SEC (SEC File No. S7-15-02) (Aug. 9, 2002) (comment letter on the Interagency White Paper on Structural Change in the Settlement of Government Securities). The value of the collateral posted exceeds the amount of cash loaned. This "haircut" or "margin" provides the lender with a buffer against short-term variations in the value of the securities. *Id.* at 5. The higher the perceived risk of the collateral, the greater the haircut. Even though a security is held as collateral in a repo, a dealer may still sell the security to a buyer in a separate transaction. Clearing banks assume an extreme amount of intraday exposure because each morning every repo transaction (even those that are not yet maturing) is "unwound" (or, perhaps more descriptively, "disassembled"). In the unwinding process, the clearing bank releases collateral securities to the dealer to permit the dealer to delivery those securities to buyers. The unwinding creates an overdraft in the dealer's account at the clearing bank, which remains in place until the dealer posts replacement collateral securities, which are then locked into the cash lender's account at the end of the day when the repo transaction is "rewound" (or reassembled). In 2010, the value of securities financed through the tri-party repo market averaged $1.7 trillion, down from a peak of $2.8 trillion in 2008. *FRBNY Repo White Paper* at 6. At its peak, individual dealers routinely financed $100 billion in securities through the tri-party repo market, with one firm (regulators aren't saying which one) financing more than $400 billion. *Payments Risk Committee Report, supra* note 55, at 3, 6, and 14.

[69] *Statement of Timothy F. Geithner, supra* note 53, at 10-11. The loan was extended by the FRBNY to JP Morgan through the discount window through the FRB's authority under Section 13(3) of the Federal Reserve Act, 12 U.S.C. 343. *Id.* at 11-13. Section 13(3) authorized the FRB, in "unusual and exigent circumstances" to authorize any Federal Reserve Bank "to discount for any individual, partnership, or corporation, notes, drafts, and bills of exchange when such notes, drafts, and bills of exchange are indorsed or otherwise secured to the satisfaction of the Federal Reserve Bank." Before making the loan the Federal Reserve Bank was required to obtain evidence that such individual, partnership, or corporation was "unable to secure adequate credit accommodations from other banking institutions." 12 U.S.C. 343. The DODD-FRANK ACT clarified and expanded the FRB's authority to lend to non-bank companies. Contemporaneous with the loan to Bear, the FRB also announced the establishment of a Term Lending Facility, which allowed primary dealers to pledge a wider range of collateral to borrow Treasury securities. *Statement of Timothy F. Geithner, supra* note 53, at 12.

repayment of the non-recourse loan, the first such financing arrangement by the U.S. Government of an entity other than a bank since the Great Depression.[70] The goal of the short-term loan was to enable Bear to open on Friday, March 14, 2008, to buy time to allow Bear and regulators to explore options with other financial institutions that would allow Bear to avoid bankruptcy or, should no such alternative be available, to allow regulators to contain the risks to the markets that a bankruptcy would cause.[71]

C. <u>Bear Continues to Sink</u>

Rather than diminish counterparty and investor anxiety about Bear, the Government credit extension only increased it. Upon news of the loan, credit rating agencies downgraded Bear.[72] Throughout the day on Friday, hedge funds and other Bear customers continued to wire staggering amounts of cash from their accounts with Bear as the firm's stock plunged.[73] After the markets closed, Treasury Secretary Henry Paulson Jr. advised Bear's Chief Executive Officer Alan Schwartz that he would need to have a deal in place to address the firm's capital deficit by Sunday night.[74]

---

[70] KELLY. *supra* note 52, at 68. The Bear bailout drew unflattering comparisons with Northern Rock PLC, which the Bank of England bailed out in September 2007 after depositors lost confidence in the bank. *See Fed Races to Rescue Bear, supra* note 47. To stave off a run on Northern Rock, the Bank of England extended an emergency line of credit, which appeared only to exacerbate depositors' concerns about the bank. Ultimately, the U.K. nationalized the bank. The scenario was also compared to the 1984 bailout of Continental Illinois National Bank and Trust Company, which the FDIC backstopped with $4.5 billion after depositors drained billions from the struggling bank, leading Bear's counsel to conclude that a financial institution can sustain a massive liquidity run only with Government intervention. *See* KELLY. *supra* note 52, at 134-135. For his part. Federal Reserve Chairman Bernanke thought the Bear crisis reminiscent of that face by Credit Anstalt, a large Austrian bank that went bankrupt in 1931 after acquiring several smaller, weaker banks. The Austrian central bank had guaranteed Credit-Anstalt's customer deposits, but the move only denigrated Austria's currency and spread panic to other European countries, contributing to the decline of Europe's banking system and the commencement of the Great Depression. KELLY, *supra* note 52, at 65. *See also Forget the Wolf Pack—the Ongoing Euro Crisis Was Caused by EMU*, Telegraph. May 16, 2010.
[71] *Statement of Timothy F. Geithner, supra* note 53, at 11.
[72] *Id.*
[73] KELLY. *supra* note 52, at 83-102.
[74] *The Fall of Bears Stearns: Bear Neared Collapse Twice in Frenzied Last Days; Paulson Pushed Low-Ball Bid, Relented; A Testy Time For Dimon*, WALL ST. J., May 29, 2008, at A1 (hereinafter "The Fall of Bear, Part 3 of 3"). Paulson and FRBNY President Geithner were concerned that Schwartz was laboring under the misconception that the loan from the FRB allowed Bear a month to seek the highest offer for the

22

Flowers and JP Morgan conducted due diligence under harried conditions that weekend.[75] On Saturday, March 15, 2008, JP Morgan notified Bear that it was considering a bid of between $8 and $12 per share for the firm, a fraction of what Bear's management believed the firm was worth.[76] JP Morgan was clear at the time, however, that it would still need to further review Bear's assets before it could make a final offer.[77]

Later that day, Flowers tentatively offered to buy 90 percent of Bear for $28 per share, a $3 billion investment. The deal was contingent, however, on Flowers lining up a consortium of lenders willing to provide $20 billion to finance Bear's continuing operations. Flowers proposed segregating some of Bear's troubled mortgage-related assets into a new security in the hopes of attracting investors who might be interested in distressed debt. The proposal also was predicated on Flowers' ability to borrow from the FRB's discount window, a move that Bear management had been advocating, unsuccessfully, for months.[78]

---

firm. From Paulson's and Geithner's perspective, it was imperative that Bear find a suitor immediately or face imminent bankruptcy. KELLY. *supra* note 52. at 101-102.

[75] Citadel, which had expressed interest in acquiring Bear. was ruled out because it was perceived as too small to close such a large deal quickly and because of lingering suspicions that the firm had been shorting Bear's stock. Bank of New York Mellon and Royal Bank of Canada each expressed interest in acquiring some portion of Bear, but neither was comfortable committing to an investment in the shaky Bear under such a short time frame. Lazard also probed interest from sovereign wealth funds (*i.e.*, investment pools controlled by foreign governments) and Santander. a large Spanish bank. For his part, Flowers contacted General Electric's GE Capital Division. the TD Bank Financial Group in Toronto. Goldman Sachs, Harvard University's endowment. and. last but not least, Warren Buffett. Other than G.E. and Goldman Sachs. which expressed some interest, the others balked. Some felt that they would not have sufficient time for due diligence. Buffett opted out. having been jaded by the industry after his bet on Salomon Brothers in 1987. He was also concerned about the optics of acquiring the once fabled firm for a song. *Id.* at 167-170, 175. Although Lazard viewed Flowers as a legitimate suitor, Paulson, who was a former Goldman Sachs colleague of Flowers' founding partner, was skeptical about a deal with Flowers because it did not have the backing of a large bank or consortium of banks. KELLY, *supra* note 52, at 129-131.

[76] KELLY. *supra* note 52, at 171.

[77] *Id.* at 173.

[78] KELLY. *supra* note 52, at 174-176. Flowers had not lined up complete financing for the deal but apparently had a commitment from GE's Capital Division to invest several billion dollars in a secured investment. *See id.* at 167 & 174. Flowers also suggested that Bear management invite Goldman Sachs to the table, which they reluctantly agree to do. *Id.* at 174-175. Goldman arrived at Bear's offices on Sunday, March 16, 2008, under a cloud of suspicion and uncertainty over what Goldman's role was to be in the process. Flowers, which invited Goldman to participate. anticipated that Goldman might have an interest in

On Sunday morning, March 16, 2008, JP Morgan withdrew its tentative offer. The bank believed that the deal was too risky given the inadequate due diligence period.[79] JP Morgan was particularly concerned about Bear's $30 billion mortgage portfolio. While Flowers' contingent offer was still pending, without committed financing, Flowers apparently was not viewed as a serious contender in the process.[80]

With no deal on the table, the FRB and Treasury concluded that an infusion of Government capital was likely the only alternative to bankruptcy for Bear.[81] The agencies decided that they could provide financing against collateral posted by Bear, but were not willing to sign off on such a deal unless it was clear that Bear's shareholders would not get a windfall if JP Morgan took over the firm with the help of Government financing.[82] Notwithstanding its concerns about Bear's mortgage portfolio, JP Morgan appeared willing to make an offer of between $3 and $5 per share for the firm. Treasury officials, however, thought a nominal price of between $1 and $2 per share was more in keeping with the policy against providing a windfall to Bear's shareholders.[83] On Sunday evening JP Morgan returned to the table, this time with a reduced offer of $4 per share,

---

buying Bear's prime brokerage business. Flowers contends that discussions between Goldman and Flowers about Goldman acquiring a part of Bear were quickly aborted when Goldman refused to sign a nondisclosure agreement because Goldman had already started to poach Bear's employees. A Goldman executive has no recollection of the nondisclosure issue. At any rate. the dispute. if any, apparently did not stop Goldman officials from seeking broader information about the firm directly from Bear. *Id.* at 200-203. Whatever Goldman's role, the firm never committed capital to any proposal to acquire Bear or any of its assets. Later that day. Bear. possibly through Flowers, contacted Morgan Stanley to determine whether it might have an interest in acquiring Bear's prime brokerage unit but. after a cursory assessment, Morgan Stanley dropped out of the process. *Id.* at 205-206.

[79] *Statement of Timothy F. Geithner. supra* note 53 at 13.

[80] KELLY. *supra* note 52, at 173, 202 & 209. While Flowers may not have been viewed as a viable contender in the process, Bear's management viewed the firm's participation as valuable because it created the appearance. if not the actuality, of a two-party bidding process.

[81] The Agencies did not believe they had the authority to acquire an equity interest in either Bear or JP Morgan. nor we they prepared to guarantee Bear's "very substantial obligations. And the only feasible option for buying time would have required open ended financing by the Fed to Bear into an accelerating withdrawal by Bear's customers and counterparties." Statement of Timothy F. Geithner, supra note 53. at 13.

[82] *Id.* at 198. *See also* Peter Robison, *Dimon Rejected Rescuing Bear Until Geithner Promised Funding,* Bloomberg, April 4, 2008.

[83] *Id.* at 204-205.

contingent upon the FRB's assumption of $30 billion of Bear losses.[84] Hours later JP Morgan revised the offer down to $2 per share. JP Morgan also agreed to guarantee Bear's obligations until the deal closed. A disgusted Bear board, believing that $2 was better than nothing, voted to approve the deal.[85] Once the fifth largest investment bank with a market value of $25 billion, the JP Morgan offer valued the firm at $243 million.[86]

The $2 offer was met with open revolt by Bear's shareholders who threatened to scuttle the deal and take their chances in bankruptcy. Moreover, due to what may have been some careless drafting, JP Morgan perhaps would have still been on the hook for guaranteeing Bear's obligation, even if the deal failed to close as a result of a no vote by Bear's shareholders.[87] The original purchase price of $2 per share for Bear was eventually raised to $10 per share for a 40% stake in the company (placing its value at $1.2 billion) to diminish the outrage expressed by Bear's shareholders after the announcement of the original terms of the deal.[88]

D. **A Trip to Maiden Lane: JP Morgan Receives Government Financing To Acquire Bear**

The FRB facilitated JP Morgan's acquisition of Bear through a $29 billion non-recourse loan that it made to a newly created limited liability company ("LLC") called "Maiden Lane," of which the FRBNY is the sole and managing member.[89] JP Morgan

---

[84] *The Fall of Bear, Part 3 of 3, supra* note.

[85] KELLY. *supra* note 52, at 208, 210.

[86] Although the perception of a windfall to Bear's shareholders was a primary concern of the Government, there apparently was no such concern with respect to JP Morgan's shareholders. After the original deal was announced, JP Morgan's stock rose 10 percent in a down market, increasing the bank's capitalization by more than $12 billion. Steven M. Davidoff, *JP Morgan's $12 Billion Bailout*, NY TIMES DealBook. March 18, 2008. A fuller understanding of the risk that JP Morgan was assuming in guaranteeing Bear's obligations—even if the deal did not close--might have tempered investor enthusiasm.

[87] Ashby Jones, *Did Deal Overexpose J.P. Morgan?*, WALL ST. J., March 25, 2008, at C2.

[88] *See id.* at 226.

[89] In New York, the FRBNY building is bordered on one side by Liberty Street and on another by Maiden Lane.

also extended a $1 billion note, subordinated to the FRBNY note, to Maiden Lane. With the proceeds of these loans, Maiden Lane purchased assets from Bear Stearns which, according to Bear, were worth $30 billion.[90] At the time Maiden Lane was established some expressed the belief that the FRB was merely buying Bear's riskiest assets, which would have otherwise appeared on JP Morgan's books. JP Morgan's CEO denied this accusation, stating that, although a confidentiality agreement constrained what he could say about the assets, the assets consist "entirely of loans that are current and domestic securities rated investment grade. We kept the riskier and more complex securities in the Bear Stearns portfolio for our own account."[91]

E.   JP Morgan Guarantees Bear's Obligations Before Deal Closes

JP Morgan agreed to guarantee certain of Bear's obligations for a certain period of time to provide stability to the markets before the Bear deal closed.[92] The scope and timing of the guarantee, however, was itself a source of uncertainty. Under the original guaranty agreement JP Morgan agreed to "unconditionally" guarantee "the due and punctual payment" of all of Bear's "covered liabilities" for the period beginning March 16, 2008, until either the deal closed or when the deal was scuttled, whichever came first. The guarantee applied to all transactions on Bear's books as of the signing of the deal in principle and any transactions entered into while the guarantee was in place. The only way for the deal to be scuttled under the agreement in a manner that would terminate JP Morgan's guarantee was for Bear's board to oppose the deal. In the absence of board

---

[90] Blackrock Financial Management Inc. manages Maiden Lane's portfolio for the FRBNY. *Maiden Lane LLC (A Special Purpose Vehicle Consolidated by the Federal Reserve Bank of New York) Consolidated Financial Statements for the Period March 14, 2008 to December 31, 2008, and Independent Auditor's Report* at note 1.

[91] Testimony of Jamie Dimon before the Senate Committee on Banking, Housing and Urban Affairs, April 3, 2008.

[92] *Statement of Timothy F. Geithner, supra* note 53, at 13-16.

opposition, JP Morgan's obligations would continue, even if Bear's shareholders voted the deal down. The coverage period was viewed as lasting at least a year and perhaps longer.[93]

The original guaranty agreement was quickly revised when the price for Bear was raised from $2 to $10 per share. Under the amended guaranty agreement, JP Morgan "unconditionally guaranties the due and punctual payment of all Covered Liabilities of" forty Bear affiliates, adding nineteen additional subsidiaries to the original agreement.[94] Obligations of Bear-sponsored special purpose entities or structured investment vehicles (*i.e.* SIVs) were not covered.[95]

Transactions the guaranty covered included: (1) all short and long-term loans; (2) all contracts associated with Bear's trading businesses; and (3) all obligations to deliver cash, securities or other property held by Bear to customers under custody arrangements. Coverage excluded, among other things: (1) Bear's bond debt and other debt securities issued by Bear; (2) employee and trade/vendor claims; (3) claims for violations of law; and (4) claims for non-contractual breach of duty.

The amended guaranty covered liabilities that arose before the Acquisition Agreement was signed. The amount guaranteed was not capped. The guaranty would terminate if Bear's board recommended a competing proposal, but only if such proposal were accompanied by an equivalent guaranty to take effect simultaneously with the

---

[93] Ashby Jones. *Did Deal Overexpose J.P. Morgan?*, WALL ST. J.. March 25, 2008, at C2. See also Statement of Timothy F. Geithner, supra note 53, at 15 ("several infirmities became evident in the agreement between JPMorgan and Bear during the week of March 17 that needed to be cured").

[94] Bear reportedly had nearly 500 subsidiaries. *See supra* note 58 and accompanying text. Therefore, the guaranty would have covered only a fraction of these. It's not clear what criteria were used in determining which subsidiaries would be included in the guaranty.

[95] Amended and Restated Guaranty Agreement and Key Terms of JPMorgan Chase Amended and Restated Guaranty Agreement Date March 16, 2008. *Compare* Statement of Timothy F. Geithner, *supra* note 53, at 14 (Government financing made it possible for JP Morgan to "step in immediately to guarantee all of Bear's short-term obligations.").

termination of JP Morgan's guaranty so that there was no gap between the guaranties. The competing guaranty would have to be given by "a financial institution with capital, liquidity and financial resources sufficient to enable Bear to conduct business in the ordinary course."[96]

F. Take-Aways From Bailout/Buyout of Bear

1. Gradual Deterioration of Bear Allowed Time for Alternatives, Most of Which Bear Rejected

Unlike LTCM, which found itself in a crisis state very quickly, warning signs of Bear's impending demise occurred over several months. From the time of the failure of Bear's hedge funds it had ample warning that its reputation as a prudent risk manager was compromised. Numerous market participants warned Bear that it needed to raise more capital. Bear had numerous suitors that would have bolstered its financial condition and possibly warded off the bailout/buyout. If Bear's shareholders had voted down the Acquisition Agreement, JP Morgan's guaranty would terminate as to new liabilities, but the guaranty of obligations guaranteed during the guaranty period would remain in effect.[97]

2. Bear's Competitors Were Also Suffering

Unlike the LTCM situation, where most of the largest brokers and banks with the financial wherewithal to make a contribution were financially strong, the difficult market conditions at the time of Bear's demise had weakened Bear largest competitors and counterparties. The firms were in self-preservation mode and reluctant to take on the added risk of Bear positions.

---

[96] Key Terms, supra note at ¶ 11.
[97] Id. at ¶ 12.

3. FRB Loan Viewed As Sign of Bear's Weakness

Key factors that affect how the markets will perceive a third-party investment in a firm include: (1) the amount of the investment; and (2) the source of the investment. In LTCM, the amount was relatively small compared to LTCM's exposure but the source, a private industry consortium) sent a message to the markets: the largest and best capitalized firms have a vested interest in ensuring that LTCM continues to trade, at least until its positions can be unwound in an orderly fashion. The FRB loan to Bear sent a much different set of messages. The amount the FRB was lending was limited only by the collateral that Bear could provide. Rather than capping the loan at a certain fixed number, the FRB loan suggested that Bear's potential was high and perhaps unknowable. The credit extension to Bear also sent a message to the markets that Bear was out of private industry options; they don't call Uncle Sam the lender of last resort for nothing. Governments don't lend to faltering private firms to make money. They invest to avert disaster. In reality, the message that Bear was out of private alternatives may have been overstated. Flowers was still interested in Bear if he could secure financing, but was unable to line it up under the short time frame. JP Morgan may also have been genuinely interested in Bear as an investment (as opposed to an obligation imposed on the bank by the FRB), but with the FRB showing its hand and apparently no other firm willing or able to take the risk, JP Morgan was able to drive a hard bargain for Bear. And with the help of Secretary Paulson may have received a windfall in the process.

4. Credit Rating Agencies' Eleventh Hour Downgrades Help Force FRB's Hand

Many have faulted the credit rating agencies' for rating mortgage-based derivative securities in a way that may not have accurately reflected the risk that those securities posed and thereby contributing to the financial crisis. Less has been written about the credit rating agencies' role in heightening an already turbulent time by downgrading securities that Bear had packaged for resale and eventually Bear itself after the FRB extended credit to Bear. The downgrade of Bear itself after the FRB extended credit is particularly noteworthy not because of the guidance that the rating agencies provided about Bear but because of the fact that the downgrades themselves triggered covenants in the debt agreements, which authorized firms that lent to Bear to call the loans immediately.[98] Triggering the debt covenants tightened the noose around Bear and may have forced the FRB's hands in pressuring Bear to reach a deal immediately rather than weigh any competing offers that may have materialized over the 28-day loan period. Although the downgrades of Bear did not provide any new information to the public they made a bad situation even worse.[99]

5. Take-Over of Bear Introduced Good Bank/Bad Bank Paradigm And The Concept of A Preclosure Guarantee

(i) Good Bank/Bad Bank Paradigm

JP Morgan determined that it could not, with limited time for due diligence, take on all of Bear's exposures, separate and apart from any financing help the FRB might provide. Moreover, from its perspective, the FRB viewed its authority under Section 13(3) of the Federal Reserve Act as limited to lending against collateral. The Maiden Lane transaction was a way to accommodate both the FRB and JP Morgan. JP Morgan was able to identify a discreet pool of assets—Bear's $30 billion real estate portfolio—that was either too risky for JP Morgan to underwrite or the risks of which were not

---

[98] *See* KELLY, *supra* note 52, at 100.

[99] As discussed in Section __ below, it may be worth examining whether anything could be gained by suspending the issuance of ratings for firms that are in the process of being reviewed by a liquidity consortium or emergency government financing.

sufficiently known for JP Morgan to prudently take on, depending on your perspective.[100]

Although the process of selecting the assets that went into Maiden Lane was overseen by

Blackrock, which the FRB retained as an adviser, little information is available about

what criteria were used to select the assets, other than the fact that they were "loans that

were current and domestic securities rated investment grade"[101] and that they were

marked to market by Bear at the time they were sold to Maiden Lane. This walling off of

risky assets created a new paradigm that was not present in the LTCM rescue but would

be predominant in the Lehman context.

(ii)   Preclosure Guaranty

The Bear acquisition also introduced the concept of the acquiring firm

guaranteeing the obligations of the distressed firm before the deal closes and potentially

for a period after the deal is scuttled by a shareholder vote by the troubled firm. Like the

other terms of the deal, the JP Morgan guaranty was drafted in a hurried fashion and

apparently at the behest of the Government as another means of restoring some

semblance of calm to the counterparties of the distressed firm. A number of points of the

JP Morgan guaranty are worth highlighting:

---

[100] In testimony following the take-over, JP Morgan's CEO, Jamie Dimon, adamantly denied that JP Morgan was shifting Bear's riskiest assets to the FRB. Testimony of Jamie Dimon before the Senate Committee on Banking, Housing and Urban Affairs, April 3, 2008 ("This transaction is not without risk for JP Morgan. We are acquiring some $360 billion of Bear Stearns' assets and liabilities. The notion that Bear Stearns' riskiest assets have been placed in the $30 billion Fed facility is simply not true....The assets taken by the Fed [to collateralize Maiden Lane LLC] consist entirely of loans that are current and domestic securities rated investment grade. We kept the riskier and more complex securities in the Bear Stearns portfolio for our own account."). Nevertheless, in August 2010, more that two years after the FRBNY took over the assets, the residential and commercial loans in the portfolio were worth about $5 billion, compared to $9.6 billion in March 2008. Serena Ng et al., *Foreclosed on—By the U.S.—With Bear Assets, Fed Balances Preserving Investment and Helping Borrowers*, WALL ST. J., Aug. 4, 2010, at C1. It is unclear how much of that loss of value is related to a continued devaluation of the real estate market or a reflection of Bear's overly optimistic marking to market of the assets before they were sold to the FRB.

[101] Dimon Testimony, *supra* note.

- The guaranty did not apply to all of Bear's obligations and affiliates. Rather, it applied only to an expressed pool of covered obligations and to an expressed list of subsidiaries. For these obligations and entities JP Morgan's liability was uncapped.[102]

- The criteria for selecting the covered subsidiaries and obligations were not defined in the guaranty agreement but apparently were designed to ensure that the acquired firm's day-to-day operations and funding arrangements could proceed in the ordinary course rather than to ensure that all obligations or entities were protected.

- Only obligations on the distressed firm's balance sheet were protected by the guaranty agreement. Off-balance sheet positions (*e.g.*, those in SIVs) were not.

- The guaranty did not preclude a competing firm from bidding on the distressed firm, but the competing firm would have to offer a similar guaranty and have the resources to reasonably meet the terms of the guaranty—presumably this precondition would have precluded many private equity firms from bidding on Bear without the backing of a large bank or insurance company willing to underwrite Bear's obligations before the deal closed.

III.   Too Big to Fail No More: Lehman Brothers, GSEs, and the Dam Breaks

---

[102] With respect to non-covered entities or obligations: "JP Morgan Chase fully expects that Bear will honor all of it obligations, whether or not guarantied. The guaranty is additional credit support to reassure customers and counterparties." Key Terms, *supra* note 95 at ¶ 9.

"We have access to Fed funds. We can't fail now." -- Richard Fuld, Lehman CEO, Summer 2008[103]

A. Weary Eyes Turn to Lehman as the Firm Scrambles for Funding

Before the ink had dried on the JP Morgan take-over of Bear, weary eyes turned to Lehman Brothers, the next smallest of the standalone investment banks.[104] Rumors began circulating that Bear's demise had been precipitated by a consortium of hedge funds that had purchased credit default swaps on Bear and then shorted Bear's stock in a classic bear raid. Regardless of the accuracy of the rumors, they created an air of apprehension among the remaining investment banks, perhaps none more so than Lehman. After the fall of Bear, Lehman's CEO Richard Fuld acknowledged to his counterpart and friend at Morgan Stanley that two large banks had stopped trading with Lehman.[105]

Despite a favorable earnings report that gave Lehman a temporary respite from the selling that permeated the market after the Bear announcement, investors became increasingly skeptical of Lehman's accounting.[106] The Treasury Department was also

---

[103] *The Weekend that Wall Street Died*, WALL ST. J.. Dec. 29, 2008. at A1. After JP Morgan's take-over of Bear, the FRB also announced that it would allow investment banks to borrow directly from the Government. KELLY, *supra* note 52, at 211.

[104] Valukas Report, *supra* note 55. at n. 5769 and accompanying text (Lehman's business model was viewed as similar to Bear's in that Lehman used high leverage, low capitalization, and had a high concentration of illiquid assets like subprime and Alt-A mortgages). As with Bear, the SEC was the primary regulator of Lehman under the CSE program discussed in *supra* note 40. Nevertheless, the heads of Treasury, the FRB, which also oversaw Lehman, and the FRBNY, which was a lender to Lehman under the FRB's discount window, all had direct communications with Lehman's CEO during this period. After the take-over of Bear, the SEC and FRBNY began on-site monitoring of Lehman's financial condition. *Id.* at nn. 5728-5730 and accompanying text.

[105] ANDREW ROSS SORKIN. TOO BIG TO FAIL: THE INSIDE STORY OF HOW WALL STREET AND WASHINGTON FOUGHT TO SAVE THE FINANCIAL SYSTEM—AND THEMSELVES 15 (2009).

[106] *See id.* at 35. *See also* "Financial Stocks Lead Wall Street Turnabout: Lehman. Goldman Sachs Earnings Top Expectations," Wash. Post, March 19, 2008, at D1 (quoting a Euro Pacific Capital executive regarding Lehman's valuations: "I still don't believe any of these numbers because I still don't think there is proper accounting for the liabilities they have on their books....People are going to find out that all these profits they made were phony."). Accounting rules relating to repos permitted Lehman to reduce its

worried about Lehman's valuations and its failure to raise capital, which many larger banks had done.[107] Treasury feared that Lehman might already be insolvent.[108] Treasury Secretary Paulson prodded Lehman to raise capital or arrange for an investment by or sale to a third party.[109] Lehman agreed that that would be advisable and, of course, considered approaching Buffett. Lehman's Fuld did not know Buffett well, so he requested that Paulson call Buffett to soften him up.[110] Fuld then called Buffett himself to feel him out about investing in Lehman. Buffett was noncommittal but promised to consider it and gave Fuld some off-the-cuff numbers that Buffett might be willing to agree to if a deal looked promising. Paulson followed up Fuld's call to Buffett with his own tepid pitch for a Buffett investment in Lehman to restore market confidence. Buffett reviewed Lehman's financial statements but found numerous issues that concerned him. When Fuld called back to discuss Buffett's off-the-cuff numbers the two realized that they had not had a meeting of the minds on what the numbers meant. To Fuld's chagrin, Buffett was asking for a far better return than Fuld had originally understood. Fuld believed the terms were unworkable and the talks were ended.[111] As with the Goldman/Buffett offer for LTCM's assets, there was a disconnect between Buffett and the bankers that prevented the parties from further exploration of a deal.

---

reported debt by $38.6 billion in the fourth quarter of 2007 and $49.1 billion and $50.38 billion, respectively. in the first two quarters of 2008. which distorted Lehman's true financial condition. *See* Jackson and Skeel. *supra* note 50, at 13-14.

[107] In the summer of 2008, Lehman had exploratory discussions with a number of strategic partners. including the Korean Development Bank, MetLife and the Investment Corp. of Dubai. During this period Lehman rejected a proposal from the KDB and term sheets from MetLife and the ICD. Valukas Report, *supra* note 55, at nn. 2189-2190 and accompanying text. The examiner, however. found no breach of duty by Lehman's officers in connection with the substance of their efforts to raise capital, attract strategic investors or spin off Lehman's commercial real estate assets. *Id.* at 611.

[108] SORKIN, *supra* note 105, at 51.

[109] Valukas Report, *supra* note 55, at n. 5769.

[110] SORKIN, *supra* note 105, at 54-55.

[111] *Id.* at 56-57.

Although Lehman did not secure financing from Buffett, it raised $4 billion by selling convertible securities to a group of investment funds,[112] but the capital raise did little to calm the markets or regulators. The Treasury Department became increasingly concerned about Lehman's viability and contacted Barclays to determine whether the U.K. bank would be interested in acquiring Lehman. Barclays explained that it was in preliminary talks to acquire UBS but might have an interest in acquiring Lehman under the right conditions.[113] While Treasury lined up potential suitors for Lehman, Lehman's CEO worked diligently to stick his foot in his mouth by conceding to a financial commentator that Lehman was taking on more leverage (Lehman's leverage exceeded 30 to 1[114]) even though his peers were deleveraging.[115] Lehman's prospects were further depressed when a respected hedge fund manager accused Lehman of failing to mark its illiquid assets to market daily as required by a new accounting interpretation.[116]

As Lehman's condition became increasingly dire, it sought funding from a range of potential suitors, including AIG, GE, and the state-owned Korean Development Bank, which was headed by a former Lehman banker. Only the Koreans showed anything more than a passing interest.[117] Meanwhile, pressure mounted for senior management changes and Lehman's chief operating officer and chief financial officer resigned.[118] In a show of desperation, Lehman pitched multiple suitors, including Morgan Stanley and Bank of America. None were interested.[119] Lehman even broached the idea of becoming a

---

[112] *Id.* at 55-57.
[113] *Id.* at 93-95.
[114] *Id.* at 81.
[115] *Id.* at 101-103.
[116] *Id.* at 104-105.
[117] *Id.* at 109, 113, and 186.
[118] *Id.* at 132.
[119] *Id.* at 192 and 198.

commercial bank, but the FRB opposed the idea for fear that the effort would alert an already wary public to Lehman's desperation.[120]

In a last ditch effort, Lehman hired investment bank Lazard to explore alternative funding sources for Lehman but Lazard's pessimism toward Lehman's condition put off Lehman's CEO. With apparently no other alternative for saving Lehman the Treasury Department orchestrated a meeting between Lehman and Bank of America to try to bring the two together in a merger. Bank of America again rejected an acquisition.[121] The Korean Development Bank remained as the only possible salvation for Lehman, but the Koreans conditioned any offer on Lehman unloading its struggling real estate holdings, a sacrifice that Lehman's CEO was unwilling to make.[122] The prospect of a Lehman bankruptcy filing loomed large as regulators began to identify the systemic risks that such a prospect raised.

To prepare for the potential fall out from a Lehman bankruptcy filing, regulators identified four specific areas of Lehman's business that might stress the global financial system: (1) Lehman's repo book; (2) its derivatives book; (3) its broker-dealer operations; and (4) its illiquid assets, including Lehman's real estate holdings and private equity investments.[123] Given Lehman's large holdings in the U.K., a Lehman liquidation promised to be a messy international affair.

B. A GSE Interlude: The Implied Government Guarantee Goes Live As Treasury Mounts A Hostile Takeover

---

[120] *Id.* at 194. *See also* Valukas Report, *supra* note 55, at n. 5802 and accompanying text (FRBNY's Geithner viewed the bank holding company idea for Lehman as "gimmicky").
[121] SORKIN, *supra* note 105, at 205.
[122] *Id.* at 213-214.
[123] *Id.* at 216.

As pressing as Lehman was for regulators in the spring of 2008, a more pressing matter pushed itself to the fore. Fannie Mae and Freddie Mac—two government sponsored enterprises ("GSEs") that were at the heart of the cratering U.S. housing market—teetered on the brink of bankruptcy.[124] The Treasury Department retained Morgan Stanley to advise the U.S. on the condition of the GSEs. Morgan Stanley determined that the GSEs would need a $50 billion capital infusion just to get their capital to 2.5% of assets—still well below the skimpy 4% required for banks.[125] To head off what was certain to be a thorny political battle over the treatment of the GSEs, which had powerful and vocal supporters and opponents,[126] Treasury Secretary Paulson decided effectively to launch a hostile take-over of the GSEs under a grant of authority Congress had given the Administration just months before. In the take-over, deemed a conservatorship, the U.S. Government acquired warrants which, if exercised, allowed the Government to acquire for a nominal sum nearly 80% of the common shares of each of the publicly traded GSEs. The Government also received senior preferred shares that pay an annual dividend of 10 percent. In return, the Government committed to invest up to $200 billion in capital to stabilize the two GSE, fifty times the amount that the LTCM consortium committed to stabilize LTCM.[127]

C.   Take-Away from Treasury's Hostile TakeOver of the GSEs

---

[124] Fannie Mae and Freddie Mac were chartered by Congress in 1938 and 1970. respectively. to help ensure a reliable and affordable supply of mortgage funds throughout the country. FHFA website accessed on March 10, 2011 (http://www.fhfa.gov/Default.aspx?Page=33).

[125] *Id.* at 222.

[126] *See, e.g.*, Eric Dash, *Fannie Mae's Offer to Help Ease Credit Squeeze is Rejected, As Critics Complain of Opportunism*, N.Y. Times, Aug. 11, 2007, at C1.

[127] James R. Hagerty et al, *U.S. Seizes Mortgage Giants; Government Ousts CEOs of Fannie, Freddie; Promises Up to $200 Billion in Capital*, WALL ST. J.. Sept. 8, 2008, at A1. *See also* SORKIN. *supra* note 105, at 228. Under the agreements, Treasury would acquire $1 billion of preferred shares in each company without providing immediate cash in exchange for the commitment to provide as much as $200 billion to the companies. Management control over the companies was given to the Federal Housing Finance Authority, the GSEs' regulator.

It is difficult to imagine a scenario under which the private sector could have mobilized funding of the magnitude required to stabilize the GSEs under such an emergency time frame. To put the commitment that the U.S. Government made in taking over the GSEs in context it may be useful to examine private company initial public offerings and loan transactions. In 2010, the Agriculture Bank of China's IPO raised a record $22.1 billion or approximately 11% of the $200 billion that the U.S. Government committed in taking over the GSEs.[128] The largest syndicated loan ever was $55 billion lined up for BHP Billiton Ltd. to use in buying Rio Tinto PLC.[129] Although the GSEs were privately traded financial institutions prior to the take-over, their Government charter and implied Government guarantee, which turned into a *de facto* guarantee, put them outside the scope of this article. An orderly winddown of the GSEs, which continues today, seems properly within the public rather than the private realm. Looking ahead, however, Congress and the President have several alternatives for dealing with the GSEs, some of which could bring the functions the GSEs perform back within the scope of this article. Therefore, it is useful to briefly discuss possible options for the GSE going forward. One alternative would be for Congress to roll the functions of the GSEs into an existing government entity. This alternative seems unlikely under the current political environment where smaller government and less public incentives for home-ownership seem favored.

Another alternative would be for Congress to liquidate the GSEs and their portfolios and the leave their functions to the private sector. It is unlikely that most commercial banks would be willing or able to carry a significant percentage of residential

---

[128] *See* Sharon Terlep et al, *GMs IPO May Raise Record Amount*, WALL ST. J., Nov. 17, 2010, at B1.
[129] David Benoit, *J.P. Morgan Flexes Its Muscle in $20 Billion Loan to AT&T*, wsjonline.com, accessed on March 22, 2011.

home loans they originate on their books. Therefore, it would not be inconceivable that the commercial banks would again rely on off-balance-sheet vehicles, such as structured investment vehicles ("SIVs") to off-load the capital risk of those loans to investors. Given the reputation that SIVs gained during the Financial Crisis, most notably with respect to Citibank, however,[130] this alternative seems problematic for--if not enticing to--banks facing newly tightened capital standards. The attractiveness for SIV-issued debt to institutional investors burned badly during the Financial Crisis remains an open question.

A third alternative would be a new special purpose bank charter. The charter could be limited to buying loans from member financial institutions (*e.g.*, banks, thrifts and credit unions), repackaging them as mortgage-backed securities, and selling them to institutional investors, as the GSEs do today. The special purpose bank could serve as a utility of sorts for the member financial institutions that originate the loans. The members could be required to ensure that the special purpose bank remained "well-capitalized" under a Basel III or other recognized standard for systemically important financial institutions, such as those that might be established by the Financial Stability Oversight Counsel under Dodd-Frank.[131] If the bank's capital level fell below the mandated level it would be required to seek additional capital from its member financial institutions. The bank could be operated as a not-for-profit organization and therefore mitigate the risk of competing with its member financial institutions, much in the same

---

[130] *See. e.g.*, Andy Kessler, *The End of Citi's Financial Supermarket*, WALL ST. J., Jan. 16, 2009 at A11.
[131] *See* 12 U.S.C. 5323. *See also Advance Notice of Proposed Rulemaking Regarding Authority to Require Supervision and Regulation of Certain Nonbank Financial Companies*, 75 FR 61653 (Oct. 6, 2010).

way that a securities clearing agency does in netting and guaranteeing its members' settled trades.[132]

D. Back to Lehman: Counterparties and Clients Pull Capital as List of Potential Suitors Dwindles

The take-over of the GSEs only increased the pressures on Lehman as JP Morgan informed Lehman that it was pulling $5 billion in collateral.[133] Lehman informed JP Morgan that it could not come up with the cash and JP Morgan advised the firm to seek an LTCM-type rescue from the Government.[134] Sensing that the end was nigh for Lehman, Goldman contacted the Treasury Department to volunteer to take some of Lehman's assets off its hands if the price was right. Treasury advised Lehman to cooperate with Goldman. Treasury also encouraged Bank of America, which had previously abandoned discussions about acquiring Lehman, to reconsider an acquisition. Treasury offered to negotiate directly with Bank of America.[135] Bank of America retained Chris Flowers, who figured prominently in the Bear Stearns take-over, to do due diligence on Bank of America's behalf and viewed Flowers as a possible acquirer of Lehman's bad bank.[136]

1. Lehman Proposes Walling Off Good Bank from Bad

As hedge funds continued to pull funds out of the sinking Lehman, Lehman continued to shop its good bank/bad bank proposal as a way to salvage the firm. Some in

---

[132] *See* Securities Exchange Act Section 17A. 15 U.S.C. 78q-1.

[133] At the time, Lehman owed JP Morgan approximately $20 billion. In addition to demanding a $5 billion payment, JP Morgan also froze $17 billion of Lehman's cash and securities. Jackson and Skeel, *supra* note 50. at 14.

[134] SORKIN, *supra* note 105. at 242-243.

[135] *Id.* at 237 & 245. Federal Reserve Board Chairman Bernanke also contacts Bank of America and reportedly agrees to help resolve certain capital issues Bank of America is having with the Federal Reserve Bank in Richmond regarding Bank of America's acquisition of Countrywide to facilitate a possible Bank of America acquisition of Lehman. *Id.* at 262.

[136] *Id.* at 267.

the industry acknowledged that such an approach might work but the proposal raised concerns about how much capital would be needed to fund the "bad" bank. At its earnings call Lehman announced before a cynical audience that it was spinning off its asset management business and its struggling commercial real estate portfolio.[137] Regulators quickly concluded that Lehman's plan was doomed.

2. As Lehman Swoons Barclays Steps up to the Plate

By September of 2008, Barclays realized that Lehman was near the end of its rope and might be an attractive target at a distressed price. Barclays conveyed its interest in Lehman to the Treasury Department but insisted that any deal be negotiated directly with the U.S. Government and be completed with financial assistance from the U.S. Bank of America reached the same conclusion, telling regulators that the U.S. Government would need to guarantee up to $40 billion in Lehman's losses. U.S. regulators indicated that no such assistance would be available but left the door open to some type of assistance— possibly through a private LTCM-type consortium.[138]

3. Barclays' Regulators Balk as a New Consortium Forms to Salvage Lehman But U.S. Funding is Off the Table

Realizing that Barclays, a U.K. bank, might be close to bidding on Lehman, Secretary Paulson's counterpart in the U.K. advised Paulson that the U.K. government has serious reservations about such an acquisition. Seeing any deal for Lehman as unlikely, U.S. regulators summoned the largest banks and informed them that no U.S.

---

[137] *Id.* at 256.

[138] *Id.* at 270-271, 279. & 300. In addition to the moral hazard involved in such an arrangement. Government assistance for a Lehman buy-out also raised the possibility of political hazard given that President Bush's cousin was employed by Lehman, as was Secretary Paulson's brother. *Id.* at 284. Lehman alums also included an SEC commissioner who was the spouse of a former FRB vice chairman. Kara Scannell, *Former SEC Official Joins Davis Polk; Navigating Issues Tied to Regulation Draws Greater Focus*, Sept. 22, 2008, WALL ST. J. at B7.

Government assistance would be forthcoming and that if Lehman was to be saved the firms would have to put together a rescue package as they had with LTCM.[139] Treasury officials inform the banks that potential suitors are considering a deal for Lehman but that the consortium must be prepared to backstop the deal by acquiring Lehman's toxic assets. In other words, the consortium is asked to acquire Badco in the event that another acquirer is willing to buy GoodCo.[140]

While the consortium met to discuss ways to value Lehman's assets, Barclays, a possible suitor for Lehman's GoodCo learned that it could not acquire Lehman without a shareholder vote, which would take 60-90 days, a U.K. corporate governance requirement that could scuttle any potential deal.[141] During that period, Barclays would have to guarantee Lehman's trade or otherwise Lehman's funding would dry up. Barclays' sought potential partners that might be willing to guarantee Lehman's trades until a deal could be completed. One likely candidate was AIG. But, unbeknownst to Barclays, AIG was facing a dangerous liquidity crisis of its own.[142] That left, of course, Warren Buffett. Politely, Buffett declined.[143] Nevertheless, Barclays drafted a deal for acquiring Lehman under which Barclays would invest $3.5 billion for Lehman's GoodCo and the consortium would use that capital to take over Lehman's troubled assets (i.e., Badco). In addition to the $3.5 billion from Lehman, the consortium would have to contribute perhaps $30 billion in additional capital to fund BadCo. Although the

---

[139] *Id.* at 302.

[140] *Id.* at 312. The unenviable position of the consortium members provoked Goldman's CEO to inquire rhetorically of Treasury: "How do we get in the other room." In other words. how do we get to acquire GoodCo while others backstop our losses. Although Treasury provided no answer a likely answer is: Get there first.

[141] Recall that JP Morgan also was required to guarantee Bear's trades even though it did not yet own the firm.

[142] *Id.* at 323.

[143] *Id.* at 325.

consortium was understandably displeased with the deal structure, they recognized that it might be the only alternative for saving Lehman.[144]

4. **Consortium Ready to Buy Bad Bank But No Takers for the Good As U.S. Decides to Pull the Plug**

Using the same risk avoidance incentive they applied with respect to the LTCM rescue, the consortium members tentatively agreed to raise the capital needed to take over BadCo. While the consortium agreed to contribute enough capital to close the deal, Barclays' acquisition of GoodCo hit a regulatory snag ostensibly because the acquisition would violate a listing standard to which Barclays, as a publicly traded company, was subjected. In the U.S., listing standards are rules adopted by the securities markets on which the listed company's shares are traded. The listing standard at issue in the Barclays instance, similar to those that apply to U.S.-listed firms, was a shareholder protection rule that required shareholder approval prior to an acquisition or guarantee of another firm's debt.[145] Had it wanted the deal to go through, the U.K. government no doubt could have formulated a waiver to the listing requirements, as U.S. regulators have done countless times for U.S.-listed firms. Nevertheless, the requirement proved a convenient means for slowing down a deal that undoubtedly made U.K. regulators nervous, particularly after they learned that Bank of America, the only other suitor for

---

[144] *Id.* at 336-337.

[145] Similar U.S. stock exchange rules were at issue with respect to JP Morgan's acquisition of Bear Stearns. Rules of the New York Stock Exchange, where Bear was listed, generally require shareholder approval before issuance of securities that are convertible into more than 20% of the outstanding shares of a listed company. The rules provide an exception, however, where the delay involved in obtaining shareholder approval would jeopardize the financial viability of the listed company. The Audit Committee of Bear's Board authorized Bear to rely on this exception in completing the JP Morgan acquisition. *See* Joint Press Release of JPMorgan Chase and Bear Stearns Announcing Amended Merger Agreement and Agreement for JPMorgan Chase to Purchase 39.5% of Bear Stearns, Press Release, March 24, 2008.

Lehman, had ended negotiations.[146] Moreover, the FSA and Barclays were particularly concerned about what appeared to be a precondition to a deal for Lehman that Barclays "guarantee" Lehman's financial obligations similar to the way in which JP Morgan provided a guarantee for Bear Stearns when it acquired it.[147] Unlike the Bear Stearns transaction, however, the U.S. government was not prepared to backstop the Lehman deal, relying preferring an LTCM-type arrangement whereby the private consortium capitalized Lehman's BadCo. Given that the capital required to rescue Lehman's Badco was perhaps ten times greater than that for LTCM and that many of the consortium members were also struggling, it is perhaps no wonder that U.K. regulators objected to Barclays providing a potentially uncapped guarantee for the obligations of a U.S. company before the deal even closed.

Without a buyer for GoodCo willing to provide a preclosure guarantee, the potential deal quickly unraveled and U.S. regulators began pressuring Lehman to file for bankruptcy. The shift in the Government's posture stunned the consortium, which apparently had already accomplished the hard part (*i.e.*, capitalizing BadCo). In hindsight, it appears somewhat baffling why U.S. regulators, when they realized that the U.K. would not sign off on a Barclays deal, did not simply adjust their mandate to the consortium to include GoodCo in the rescue plan. If the consortium itself were not willing or able to take on GoodCo, then presumably independent investors—Christopher Flowers comes to mind—would have been more than happy to invest in Lehman's most valuable assets without taking on any of its riskiest real estate holdings. Indeed, it was the very deal that the Korean Development Bank argued for before Lehman's CEO killed

---

[146] Confusion over which U.S. regulator, Treasury or the SEC, was responsible for facilitating the issue with the U.K. only made matters worse. *Id.* at 344-347.

[147] Valukas Report, *supra* note 55, at n. 5939 and accompanying text.

the negotiations. That left only the matter of the guarantee. Certainly, the consortium of banks that were willing to rescue Lehman's GoodCo were in a much better position to understand the potential risks of guaranteeing Lehman's assets until the deal closed. Moreover, as unpalatable as it may have been to the U.S. Government, extending Maiden Lane-type financing to the consortium (or the U.S. contingent thereof) likely would have been at least marginally more defensible than extending it to Barclays, a U.K. bank.

But alas, it was not meant to be. Under pressure from U.S. regulators Lehman filed for bankruptcy.[148] Lehman's U.S. broker-dealer was permitted to continue trading out of its positions, but Lehman's affiliates in Europe and Asia were forced to cease operations immediately.[149] This action had a ripple effect for hedge funds that had collateral with those affiliates. Because Lehman had rehypothecated (*i.e.*, reloaned) the hedge fund collateral when the Lehman affiliates ceased operations, it was a monumental task to determine who owned what assets. With the hedge fund collateral locked up, the hedge funds were forced to sell their most liquid assets at deflated prices and began withdrawing collateral from other banks.[150] The resulting market swoon only

---

[148] On Sunday, September 14, 2008, "the SEC, with the support of the FRBNY and Treasury, all but directed Lehman to declare bankruptcy." Valukas Report, *supra* note 55, at n. 2202 and accompanying text. Lehman's holding company parent and a number of its U.S. affiliates filed for Chapter 11 bankruptcy on September 15, 2008. Lehman's U.K. broker-dealer filed for administration in the U.K. Lehman's U.S. broker-dealer operated until September 19, 2008, when it was placed into a liquidation under the Securities Investor Protection Act. "The Orderly Liquidation of Lehman Brothers Holdings Inc. under the Dodd-Frank Act," 5 FDIC Quarterly at nn. 16-17 and accompanying text (2011).

[149] This fact may have been due more to the way in which Lehman was structured than to the regulations of European and Asian regulators. For example, Lehman's European affiliate was financed entirely by the Lehman parent holding company out of New York. All liquidity ran through the parent. Once Lehman's parent filed for bankruptcy it stopped funding its European affiliate, which was taken into administration by U.K. regulators because of inadequate capitalization. *Id.* at nn. 5987-5991.

[150] *Id.* at 393-394. *See also* Jeffrey McCracken, *Lehman's Chaotic Bankruptcy Filing Destroyed Billions in Value*, WALL ST. J., Dec. 29, 2008, at A10 (The bankruptcy filing by Lehman Holdings triggered a cascade of defaults at Lehman subsidiaries that held trading contracts, which created an "event of default" for Lehman's derivatives. The default resulted in the termination of over 80% of transactions with Lehman counterparties, including contracts in which Lehman was owed money. Losses from derivatives and related claims cost Lehman's unsecured creditors at least $50 billion.) Lehman's filing had an immediate adverse impact on its creditors, few more severe than Reserve Primary Fund, a $62 billion money market

---

exacerbated the liquidity crisis at AIG, which had a hole in its $1 trillion balance sheet that was more of the GSE than the Lehman magnitude. In less tumultuous times AIG with its steady flow of premiums likely could have weathered the storm with a private sector bridge loan until the commercial paper market stabilized. In the post-Lehman filing environment, however, where short-term financing was strained for even the strongest non-financial firms (*e.g.*, McDonald's), AIG was left with no options other than a GSE-type Government take-over or a bankruptcy filing. After quick but careful consideration, AIG's board determined that 20% of something (the share that the Government would leave to shareholders after the take-over) was better than 100% of nothing (the share the Board feared would be left after a bankruptcy filing) and AIG was off to Maiden Lane.[151]

In the end, Merrill Lynch was swallowed by Bank of America for what in hindsight appears to be a generous premium, leaving only Goldman and Morgan Stanley as free-standing investment banks, both of which chose to subject themselves to regulation as bank holding companies to gain the ability of permanent access to the FRB's discount window and financing in the form of federally insured customer deposits. One of the few winners was, of course, Warren Buffett, who finally found a financial

fund that held $785 million of Lehman's commercial paper. After Lehman's filing, investors fled the fund, redeeming $40 billion in two days. The Fund subsequently "broke the buck," repricing its shares at $0.97 and causing hysteria among investors in the normally super safe investment. *See* "The Orderly Liquidation of Lehman Brothers Holdings Inc. under the Dodd-Frank Act," *supra* note 148, at nn. 19-20 and accompanying text.

[151] AIG actually took two trips to Maiden Lane. In addition to the $85 billion credit facility which the FRBNY extended directly to AIG, the Government also lent $37.8 billion to a special purpose vehicle to bail out AIG's securities lending business (Maiden Lane II) and $24.3 billion to bail out AIG's unregulated over-the-counter derivatives business (Maiden Lane III). *See* Testimony of FRB Vice Chairman Donald L. Kohn Regarding American International Group Before the Committee on Banking, Housing, and Urban Affairs, U.S. Senate, March 5, 2009. AIG also borrowed $14 billion from the FRB's Commercial Paper Funding Facility, a separate facility that the Government set up to prop up the nation's commercial paper market. For all of 2008, AIG lost $99 billion, $62 billion in the fourth quarter alone. *Id.*

firm he felt comfortable investing in—Goldman Sachs—at a bargain price that not even

Buffett could resist. Along the way, both Morgan and Goldman sought desperation

funding from the likes of the Chinese Investment Corp. and the Industrial and

Commercial Bank of China, among others.[152]

E. Take-Aways from the Lehman Bankruptcy

- ### Lehman Could Have Been Saved

There were a number of reasons why Lehman went bankrupt. One had to do with

the fact that the Government did not believe it had the legal authority to

recapitalize Lehman as it had helped to do with Bear. Chairman Bernanke told

the Lehman bankruptcy examiner: "I speak for myself, and I think I can speak for

others, that at no time did we say 'We could save Lehman but we won't.' Our

concern was about the financial system, and we knew the implications for the

greater financial system would be catastrophic, and it was."[153] Chairman

Bernanke did not believe that the FRB had the legal authority to bail out Lehman

because he did not believe that the FRBNY could lend to Lehman because

---

[152] *Id.* at 445 and 456.

[153] Valukas Report, *supra* note 55. at n. 5838 and accompanying text. Although Chairman Bernanke himself was concerned that the impact of Lehman's failure would be severe. others thought it would be less so. *See id.* at nn. 5839-5841 and accompanying text (Chairman Bernanke recalled there being a "range of views" on the likely severity of the impact of Lehman's collapse. Some believed it would be "a minor disruption" (*i.e.*, 1-15 on a scale of 1-100) and others, including Chairman Bernanke. believed it would be in the 90-95 range. The actual effect turned out to be "maybe 140…worse than almost anybody expected.").

Lehman had no collateral to secure such a loan.[154] Treasury Secretary Paulson concurred.[155]

The reasons for Lehman's failure, in my view, did not necessarily preclude a private sector rescue of the firm. Unlike the GSEs and AIG, which had dug such large holes that it would have been nearly impossible to raise the amount of capital needed to save them privately under crisis timing, Lehman could have been rescued by the private sector. In committing to capitalize BadCo with $33 billion, the consortium was already most of the way there. Raising the remaining $3.5 billion to include Lehman's GoodCo in the deal was doable, either within the consortium membership or through a side deal with a hedge fund or a sovereign wealth fund. The main sticking point for Barclays and its U.K. regulators appeared to be an insistence on the part of U.S. regulators that Barclays guaranty Lehman's obligations much in the same way that JP Morgan guaranteed Bear's. Whereas the U.S. government was willing to provide $30 billion to finance the Bear acquisition, it was, at least openly, unwilling to provide such financing to Barclays. U.S. regulators may have considered and rejected an all-consortium deal for Lehman, with or without Maiden Lane financing, but I could find no public record of such deliberations.

---

[154] *Id.* at nn. 5831-5833. In July 2008. staff at the FRBNY developed a "Maiden Lane type vehicle" for Lehman, similar to the one used to rescue Bear. Under the proposal, a special purpose vehicle would be created to take $60 billion in illiquid assets off of Lehman's books. The assets would have been backstopped by $5 billion in Lehman equity. The FRBNY ultimately decided not to extend the Maiden Lane vehicle to Lehman. *See id.* at nn. 5814-5821. FRBNY President Geithner concurred that there was nothing that the FRBNY could have done at the time to save Lehman. *Id.* at n. 5822 and accompanying text.

[155] *Id.* at n. 5849 and accompanying text. Paulson distinguished Lehman from Bear because unlike Bear, which had a "willing" buyer in JP Morgan, Lehman did not. Given that JP Morgan was unwilling to invest in Bear until the FRB committed to provide $30 billion in financing and remove Bear's risky real estate portfolio from Bear's balance sheet, *see supra* notes 82 to 84 and accompanying text, it does beg the question of what it means to be a "willing" buyer.

- **Lehman's Liquidation Should Have Been Managed Better**

Lehman's failure sent a clear message to the markets and to financial firms that they could not rely on the Government to bail them out. In that regard, the failure may have achieved short-lived public policy benefits.[156] These benefits alone, however, do not, in my estimation, justify the great wealth destruction that the way in which the bankruptcy was carried out, much of which was borne by entities with no connection to Lehman. By one estimation, as much as $75 billion of Lehman's value was destroyed by the unplanned and chaotic bankruptcy filing.[157] An executive of the advisory firm that manages Lehman's estate stated: "While I have no position on whether or not the federal government should have provided further assistance to Lehman, once the decision was made not to provide further assistance, an orderly wind-down plan should have been pursued. It [the chaotic liquidation] was an unconscionable waste of value."[158]

While reasonable people may disagree over whether Lehman should have been allowed to fail, few would argue that the process by which that failure occurred was necessary or productive. I suspect that much of the blame for the ugliness of the process (and the resulting costs) can be attributed to the fact that regulators responsible for making the ultimate call about Lehman's future had few attractive alternatives for addressing the problem. One regulatory agency noted that at the time of Lehman's failure "there was no common or adequate statutory

---

[156] Assertions that Lehman's failure struck a blow against moral hazard are undercut by the fact that prior to the bankruptcy filing the NYFRB lent Lehman over $46 billion in an effort to prop up the firm. In the subsequent sale of Lehman to Barclays, the NYFRB was paid back in full, much to the chagrin of other creditors who stand to recoup "dimes on the dollar." McCracken & Spector, *Lehman's Legacy: Fed Draws Court's Eyes in Lehman Bankruptcy*, WALL ST. J., Oct. 2, 2009, at C1.

[157] *See* McCracken, *supra* note 150, at A10.

[158] *Id.*

scheme for the orderly liquidation of a financial company whose failure could adversely affect the financial stability of the United States."[159] In Title II of the Dodd-Frank, Congress enacted such a scheme. While this statutory scheme and the agency rules promulgated under it will surely go a long way to provide regulators with the needed tools to address future instances of financial firm failures, the scheme does not, in my view, preclude the need for a formalized alternative private-sector approach. Indeed, certain provisions of the statutory scheme could make such a private-sector approach all the more appealing. For this reason it is worthwhile to consider the formulation of a regulatory structure to facilitate private sector rescues of distressed non-bank financial firms. Therefore, below I propose a private-sector alternative to the Dodd-Frank liquidation scheme that could serve as a prudent regulatory structure to facilitate such a private-sector rescue.

IV.   Dodd-Frank Orderly Liquidation Framework

A thorough analysis of the Dodd-Frank Act orderly liquidation provisions is beyond the scope of this article.[160] Nevertheless, it is important to understand the basic

---

[159] FDIC Notice Regarding Orderly Liquidation Authority Provisions of the Dodd-Frank Wall Street Reform and Consumer Protection Act, 76 FR 4207. 4208 (Jan. 25, 2011).

[160] Professor David Skeel provides one in THE NEW FINANCIAL DEAL: UNDERSTANDING THE DODD-FRANK ACT AND ITS (UNINTENDED) CONSEQUENCES (2011). Put mildly. Professor Skeel. who advised Congressional staff on the drafting of the DFA. is not a fan of the new law. He contends that the new law "enshrines a system of ad hoc interventions by regulators that are divorced from basic rule-of-law constraints." *Id.* at 9. He is particularly critical of the orderly liquidation provisions. Professor Skeel implies that the DFA threshold for taking over a struggling bank is too low and that once the institution is in government hands the FDIC can pick and choose which creditors will get paid in full and which will be left with the dregs. *Id.* at 152. Although he finds "the overall pattern of the legislation disturbing" he believes that "a handful of its contributions [the new framework for clearing derivatives and

structure of the framework as well as certain limitations in it that may warrant the development of the type of private sector alternative that this article advocates.

Prior to enactment of the DFA, "there was no common or adequate statutory scheme for the orderly liquidation of a financial company whose failure could adversely affect the financial stability of the United States."[161] Instead, there were several different liquidation frameworks that applied depending on the type of institution that was to be liquidated.

- Insured depository institutions were subject to an FDIC-administered receivership under the Federal Deposit Insurance Act.

- Insurance companies were subject to insolvency proceedings under state law.

- Registered broker-dealers were subject to the U.S. Bankruptcy Code and proceedings under the Securities Investor Protection Act.

- Other companies (including parent holding companies of any of the above) were "eligible to be a debtor under the U.S. Bankruptcy Code."[162]

These disparate insolvency regimes were found to be "inadequate to effectively address the actual or potential failure of a financial company that could adversely affect economic conditions or financial stability in the United States."[163] Rather than attempt to consolidate or harmonize the diverse and many regimes, the DFA added another in Title

---

trading them on exchanges and the new Consumer Financial Protection Bureau] could genuinely improve the regulatory landscape." *Id.* at 14.

[161] 76 FR at 4208.
[162] *Id.*
[163] *Id.*

II of the DFA. The new liquidation authority is intended to provide the FDIC with the same type of powers it already possesses with respect to commercial banks.[164]

Many of the provisions remain controversial and their application will no doubt prove to be politically sensitive. However, the process is as follows:

(1)   Predetermination by regulators of which financial institutions are systemically important;

(2)   Recommendation by the FRB and the FDIC that the Treasury Secretary appoint the FDIC as receiver for a systemically important financial institution that is in default or in danger of default (the recommendation must be made with the SEC (for a broker-dealer or an entity whose largest U.S. subsidiary is a broker-dealer) or the Director of the new Federal Insurance Office (for an insurance company or an entity whose largest U.S. subsidiary is an insurance company);[165]

(3)   Determination by the Treasury Secretary (in consultation with the President), based on certain findings, that the financial company should be placed into receivership.[166]

---

[164] *See* Jackson and Skeel, *supra* note 50 at 45.

[165] DFA § 203.

[166] DFA § 203(b). The findings that must form the basis of the determination are: (1) the company is in default or in danger of default; (2) the failure of the company and its resolution under other applicable federal or state law would have "serious adverse effects on financial stability" in the United States; (3) no viable private sector alternative is available to prevent the default; (4) effects on the interests of the company's creditors, counterparties and shareholders, and other market participants is "appropriate" given the impact that any action taken under these provisions of the DFA would have on financial stability in the United States; (5) any action taken pursuant to the FDIC's appointment as receiver (DFA § 204) would avoid or mitigate such adverse effects (taking into consideration the effectiveness of the action in mitigating potential adverse effects on the financial system, the costs of the general fund to the Treasury and the potential to increase excessive risk taking by creditors, counterparties and shareholders of the company (*i.e.*, moral hazard)); (6) a federal regulatory agency has ordered the company to convert all of its convertible debt instruments that are subject to the regulatory order; and (7) the company must meet the DFA definition of a "financial company" under DFA § 201. Subparagraph (6) apparently relates to a provision in DFA § 165(c) that authorizes the FRB to issue regulations that require nonbank financial companies that the FRB supervises and certain bank holding companies to maintain a certain amount of contingent capital that is convertible to equity in times of financial stress. Under the DFA, a "financial company" is a (i) bank holding company, (ii) a nonbank financial company supervised by the FRB, (iii) any

After determining that a financial company satisfies the criteria for receivership, the Secretary must notify the FDIC and the financial company.[167] The company's board of directors may consent in or acquiesce to the appointment of the FDIC as receiver.[168] If it does, the Secretary may make the appointment without going to court. If the board does not consent or acquiesce, then the Secretary must petition the U.S. District Court for the D.C. Circuit for an order authorizing the appointment.[169] The court's review of the Secretary's determination is limited to whether it was arbitrary and capricious for the Secretary to find that the financial company is "in default or in danger of default"[170] and that the company satisfies the DFA's definition of "financial company."[171] If the court determines that the Secretary's determination with respect to these two findings was not arbitrary and capricious, then it will authorize the Secretary to appoint the FDIC as receiver.[172]

The FDIC's authority as receiver under the DFA is provided in section 204, which highlights that it is the purpose of the orderly liquidation provisions to "provide the necessary authority to liquidate failing financial companies that pose a significant risk to the financial stability of the United States in a manner that mitigates such risk and minimizes moral hazard."[173] To the extent that fair treatment of creditors or customers of the failing firm are to be considered in carrying out the liquidation authority, they are

---

company that is "predominantly engaged in" activities that the FRB has determined are financial in nature or incidental thereto (other than (i) or (ii)); (iv) any subsidiary of (i) through (iii) that the FRB determines is predominantly engaged in activities that are financial in nature or incidental thereto (other than an insured depository institution or an insurance company) (Farm Credit Systems are excluded from the definition).
[167] DFA § 202(a)(1)(A)(i).
[168] Board members are not liable to the financial company's shareholders or creditors for acquiescing or consenting in good faith to the appointment of the FDIC as receiver. DFA § 207.
[169] DFA § 202(a)(1)(A)(i).
[170] This term is defined in DFA § 203(c)(4).
[171] See DFA § 202(a)(1)(A)(iii).
[172] DFA § 202(a)(1)(A)(iv)(II). If the court does not rule within 24 hours of receiving the Secretary's petition, then the petition shall be granted "by operation of law." DFA § 202(a)(1)(A)(v).
[173] DFA § 204(a).

clearly subordinate under the DFA to the twin goals of mitigating financial stability risk and minimizing moral hazard. To that end, Congress is clear that the FDIC must exercise its authority so that:

(1) shareholders and creditors will bear the financial company's losses;

(2) management responsible for the failure of the financial company will not be retained; and

(3) the FDIC (and other applicable agencies) will take all steps "necessary and appropriate" to assure that all parties responsible for the failing firm's condition will bear the losses.[174] Such action may include restitution, actions for damages and recoupment of compensation.

The DFA leaves scant room for innocent bystanders and victims of circumstances. If a company is in default or risks default and is important enough to pose a significant risk to the financial stability of the United States, then heads will roll.

Moreover, the DFA and the FDIC's interpretation of it are clear that the DFA permits the FDIC to pay certain creditors of a receivership more than similarly situated creditors if the FDIC deems such action is necessary to: (1) maximize the value of (or minimize the loss from the sale of) assets; and (2) initiate and continue operations of the receivership and any bridge financial company.[175] To be sure, the FDIC has provided assurance that only a "limited group" of creditors would be entitled to additional

---

[174] DFA § 204(a)(1)-(3).

[175] See DFA §§ 210(b)(4), (d)(4) and (h)(5)(E) and 76 FR at 4211. The DFA authorizes the FDIC to transfer certain contracts of the failing firm (e.g., securities contracts, repos, and swaps) to a new entity such as a bride financial company to avoid termination of those contracts. The Orderly Liquidation of Lehman Brothers Holdings Inc., supra note 148, at nn. 30-31 and accompanying text. According to the FDIC, "[t]he bridge financial company is a completely new entity that will not be saddled with the shareholders, debt. senior executives or bad assets and operations that led to the failure of the covered financial company." 76 FR at 4209. The authority to charter a bridge financial company, authority similar to that the FDIC has under the FDIA with respect to insured depository institutions, is reminiscent of the GoodCo/BadCo structure that the private consortium considered as a way to wall off Lehman's good assets from its bad.

payments under the DFA's "strict standards," that certain categories of creditors would never be entitled to such additional payments (*e.g.*, creditors holding certain unsecured senior debt with a term more than 360 days), and that, at a minimum, creditors under the DFA liquidation provisions will receive no less than the creditor would have under Chapter 7 of the Bankruptcy Code.[176] Nevertheless, the FDIC concedes that the orderly liquidation authority under the DFA would be a remedy of last resort to be used only after other remedies are unable to stave off failure. The FDIC anticipates that the mere knowledge of the consequences of a Title II resolution would encourage a struggling firm to find an acquirer or partner prior to a failure.[177] Indeed, the DFA requires the Secretary to determine whether such private sector alternatives are available before deciding whether the FDIC should be appointed as receiver.[178] Therefore, I turn now to one such possible alternative.

V.   Regulatory Framework to Facilitate Private Sector Rescues of Distressed Non-Bank Financial Firms—A Liquidity Consortium Approach

The LTCM rescue and the Financial Crisis of 2007-2008 clearly show that from time to time there will be a need to access, on an emergency basis, a substantial amount of capital to avert far greater capital destruction and the resulting loss of investor confidence. The capital might be necessary to facilitate an orderly winddown of the firm in a manner that is most efficient in terms of minimizing wealth destruction or the capital infusion may make it possible for the firm's rehabilitation, either as a whole or in parts.

---

[176] 76 FR at 4211. The FDIC's guidance about how it will likely interpret the DFA liquidation priorities appears intended to address lingering concerns that those provisions may be applied in a manner that unfairly favors short-term creditors over long-term creditors of the failing financial firm in the name of promoting financial stability. *See, e.g.*. Skeel, *supra* note 160 ("[i]f regulators do take over a large financial institution under their resolution authority, they can evade the bankruptcy-like provisions by simply agreeing to pay favored creditors in full under the FDIC's carte blanche to cherry-pick among creditors").
[177] *See* "The Orderly Liquidation of Lehman Brothers Holdings Inc," *supra* note 148 at 19.
[178] DFA § 203(b)(3).

Regulatory means are in place under the FDIA to address a failing bank or other insured depository institution. Moreover, under the DFA, a heretofore untested mechanism is in place to isolate the impact of a failure of a systemically important non-bank, which emphasizes loss absorption by creditors and shareholders of that entity. Such a structure was politically feasible at the time the law was enacted, but it is at best a last ditch approach for unwinding a troubled firm that has no other viable alternative for saving itself. Now that the crisis that gave rise to the DFA has dissipated, critics of the DFA generally and of the liquidation provisions specifically have gained momentum. Unlike the FDIA provisions for liquidating insured depository institutions, which provide the popular safeguard of guaranteeing customer deposits, the benefits of the DFA provisions are much more tenuous from the perspective of an average citizen, thereby making the DFA provisions more susceptible to efforts to roll them back. Whether or not critics of the DFA prove successful in repealing or significantly diluting the liquidation provisions, in either case the end result will be an imperfect means for addressing the likely future occurrence of the failure of a systemically important financial firm. Therefore, it is worthwhile to discuss alternative approaches to addressing such a failure.

As experience with LTCM suggests, a private sector consortium has the ability to put in place in a short time frame the means to raise sufficient capital to facilitate the orderly winddown of a large troubled financial firm. Arguably, such a framework was well on its way toward facilitating an orderly winddown of Lehman and could have completed the task had U.S. regulators been willing to show some flexibility in backstopping the transaction. The sticking point—the insistence on a preclosure guarantee of certain of Lehman's obligations—had it been vetted and sized in advance, might have proven far less daunting to potential liquidity providers such as hedge funds and sovereign wealth funds, than it appeared to Barclays and its U.K. regulators.[179] Ultimately, the guarantee was nothing more than a short-term insurance policy to comfort Lehman's counterparties and creditors to assure them that the sky would not fall from the time a consortium inked a deal until the deal closed. After an initial drafting hiccup with respect to the drafting of the JP Morgan/Barclay's guarantee, the guarantee itself appeared to cause little concern for JP Morgan's stakeholders who viewed the bank as landing a sweetheart deal. If U.S. regulators were concerned about a potential Lehman consortium taking on the additional risk of a guarantee, it is not difficult to imagine a separate side deal between the consortium and other liquidity providers, a few of whom had already done the due diligence on Lehman, taking on the guarantee in the form of a swap.

I believe that such a framework could have worked effectively to preserve Lehman and avoid much of the fall-out from its liquidation. Nevertheless, ad hoc consortia, particularly those facilitated through emergency government action, run the risk of being perceived as government bail-outs, which undercut the usefulness of the framework. The ad hoc approach used with LTCM raises a number of concerns, such as the free rider problem illustrated by Bear Stearns' non-participation. Moreover, an ad

---

[179] Of course, investments from sovereign wealth funds raise their own unique set of concerns. A study of sovereign wealth fund investment patterns highlighted some of these concerns. Bernardo Bortolotti, Veljko Fotak, William Meggison, and William Miracky, "Sovereign Wealth Fund Patterns and Performance" (2009). The study examined 33 funds that control assets of over $2 trillion. Fourteen of the funds were created after 2004. Most of this growth was fueled by petroleum-related trade surpluses earned by state-owned enterprises primarily based in non-Western, non-democratic countries. Their investments were typically large, risky, and cross-border, and often were concentrated in such politically sensitive areas as banking, energy, and telecommunications. American companies attracted about half of all investments from sovereign wealth funds and about one third of the total value ($58.3 billion of $181.6 billion invested). Much of this investment was focused on U.S. financial companies. Although sovereign wealth fund investors tend to be long-term investors, they are typically poor at monitoring management and may even exacerbate conflicts between management and minority shareholders by freeing management from effective oversight, often because of the perception of the sovereign funds medaling in foreign operations. A recent high-profile case underscored the thorny issues that such investments raise. Margaret Coker and Liz Rappaport, *Libya's Goldman Dalliance Ends in Losses, Acrimony*, WALL ST. J., May 31, 2011, at A.1.

hoc approach that is facilitated by the government, will be open to criticism that the government should not be dictating which firms should be rescued (and on what terms) and which should be allowed to fail.

Finally, an ad hoc approach, by definition, allows no formalized means for accessing potential liquidity, such as capital from hedge funds, the offers of which during the Financial Crisis of 2007-2008 often raised suspicion from distressed firms which feared (sometimes justifiably) that the hedge fund was merely bottom fishing or seeking information upon which it could build a short position to drive the target firm's stock lower. A formalized regulatory approach could help address these concerns.

A.   How a Liquidity Consortium Might Work

The liquidity consortium approach I envision would be a bundle of rights and responsibilities that would apply to private firms that might be willing and able to participate in a liquidity consortium assembled for the purpose of recapitalizing or facilitating the winding down of a struggling non-bank financial firm. For simplicity I will refer to this bundle of rights and responsibilities as Regulation LC (or Reg LC) for liquidity consortium.

Reg LC would establish, among other requirements, eligibility criteria for consortium members. Membership could be two-tiered, one set of criteria for LC "sponsors" and another for members that are not sponsors. The base membership requirement could recognize firms based on financial sophistication. A number of existing economic sophistication standards could be adapted for this purpose.[180]

---

[180] For example, firms that wished to be consortium members might be required to meet the same sophistication standards as those required of "major U.S. institutional investors" or "qualified institutional buyers" as those terms are defined under the U.S. securities laws. *See* Securities Exchange Act of 1934 Rule 15a-6 (17 CFR § 240.15a-6(a)(4) (entities that have or have under management total assets in excess

At least one member of the consortium would be required to meet the stricter standards of a LC "sponsor." The sponsor would be the party legally responsible for meeting the requirements of the LC designation. In other words, the sponsor would be the regulator "hook" on the consortium. I would envision that banks, broker-dealers, and other regulated financial institutions that met the financial sophistication requirements could serve as consortium members and as sponsors. Hedge funds, other private equity firms, and non-U.S. financial institutions (including sovereign wealth funds) could qualify as LC members so long as they met the financial sophistication requirements, but not as sponsors.

The LC process could be invoked by the sponsor filing a notice with the Treasury Department (or other appropriate regulatory agency) notifying the government that an LC had been formed with respect to a particular target firm. The filing would identify the target firm, whether it was publicly traded, and whether it was regulated and by whom. The filing would identify all members of the consortium and represent that all members meet whatever criteria are established to be such a member. The filing could also include an explanation of why a liquidity consortium is appropriate for this firm (*e.g.*, that the company was in default or in danger of default).

The sponsor could also be required to represent that it had segregated a certain amount of "good faith" capital to ensure that it had sufficient "skin in the game" to facilitate a recapitalization or winding down of the distressed firm.[181] If a preclosure guarantee was deemed necessary, the sponsor could also represent that it was prepared to

---

of $100 million) and Securities Act of 1933 Rule 144A (17 CRF § 230.144A(a)(1) (entities that own and invest at least $100 million in securities of unaffiliated issuers).

[181] The filing of an LC notice (and good faith deposit or segregation) should not, in my view, preclude consortium members from betting against the target firm, so long as filing the LC notice was not done merely with the intent of gathering information to undermine the struggling firm.

make the necessary guarantee if an agreement between the consortium and the struggling firm was reached.

B. Possible Incentives For Establishing an LC

With respect to LTCM and the many financial entities that struggled during the Financial Crisis of 2007-2008, the government determined that it was beneficial for U.S. market stability to form a private liquidity consortium. Unlike the Financial Panic of 1907, where J. Pierpont Morgan raced back from Richmond, Virginia to New York, to mobilize his counterparts to quell the liquidity crunch, no private sector individual— sadly, not even Warren Buffett —played the same proactive leadership role in calming the markets.[182] Valuable time and assets were wasted in the time from the start of the crisis until the government stepped in to direct the formation of a consortium. Therefore, it could be beneficial to provide certain incentives that would make it more likely for firms to proactively form liquidity consortiums before being directed or encouraged to do so by the government. The filing of the LC notice discussed above could trigger these benefits.

Filing the LC notice could entitle LC members to the benefits that could include:

--suspension of short selling rules for target company shares, which many of the struggling firms blamed for the speed of their demise;[183]

--moratorium on rating agency downgrades (which can trigger collateral calls);

--exemptions from antitrust laws for consortium members;

---

[182] For a detailed and timely treatment of the 1907 crisis, *see* ROBERT F. BRUNER AND SEAN D. CARR, The Panic of 1907: Lessons Learned from the Market's Perfect Storm (2009).

[183] *See, e.g.*, Patrick Fitzgerald and Mike Spector, *Lehman: Och-Ziff Helped Spread Rumors*, WALL ST. J., Aug. 13, 2010, at C4.

--special tax treatment for any resulting deal done through the auspices of the LC structure;

--right of first refusal should a competing bidder surface; and

--access to public financing under certain limited circumstances and with respect to certain struggling entities. Such financing could include LC sponsor access to the FRB's discount window during the period from the announcement of a deal until the deal closes, a period during which, if the sponsor agreed to a preclosure guaranty, the sponsor would be on the hook for the struggling firm's trades.

Any government involvement in the rescue of a struggling firm will, of course, raise the specter of a bail-out. That is why a liquidity consortium model must carefully prescribe and target government involvement. In this regard, the government's role would be limited to:

--dictating disclosure requirements for LC sponsors;

--administering transaction-specific regulatory safe harbors (*e.g.*, antitrust exemption, short selling suspension, and credit rating suspensions);

--authorizing credit extensions in limited circumstances

   --where failure of target in the context of existing market conditions would likely result in systemic risk;

   --to obtain a credit extension the LC sponsor must already be authorized to access the Discount Window;

   --Credit extensions would require a determination consistent with FRB Regulation A (section 201.4(b), *i.e.*, secondary credit) that such credit was necessary to facilitate the orderly resolution of the serious financial difficulty of the struggling firm.

Risk of loss would ultimately have to be borne by the liquidity consortium and underwritten by the LC sponsor.

C.   Benefits of a Liquidity Consortium Approach

The liquidity consortium approach provides a number of possible benefits. These include:

--Establishing prequalified sources of capital;

--Promoting regulatory accountability by delimiting regulatory involvement;

--Preserving capital and jobs by providing breathing room for the distressed firm to facilitate a deal or wind down in an orderly manner;

--Providing a mechanism for attracting private sources of liquidity may help to prevent the crisis from worsening; and

--Postponing and potentially avoiding the uncertain and potentially draconian alternative of a resolution under the DFA orderly liquidation provisions. The filing of an LC notice could serve as an informal stay of the DFA liquidation process.

D.   What likely message would participation of a Liquidity Consortium send to the markets?

While the LC notice could be allowed to be filed without disclosure to the public (at least for a limited time), it is unrealistic to assume that the markets will not be alerted to the fact that a consortium is being formed. Therefore, it is important to consider the potential message that the formation of such a consortium would send to the markets

62

regarding the struggling firm. Recall that the initial government financing for Bear only expedited the firm's decline, whereas news of a potential investment from Buffett buoyed Goldman Sachs.

The message that the formation of an LC would send depends on the perceived motivation of the members (*e.g.*, is the consortium a surrogate for a government-funded bail-out (*e.g.*, JPM take-over of Bear) or a market-driven assessment of the distressed firm)? The message would also be impacted by the perceived reasons for the LC formation. For example, is the failure of the firm a systemic threat? Is it a strategic fit for an LC member? Is it a good investment opportunity for a savvy investor? Ultimately, the message will be dictated by the circumstances. A potential factor that might suggest that the message will tend to be more positive than negative, all things being equal, is that the filing of an LC notice might suggest to the markets that the more uncertain process of a DFA liquidation will be delayed and potentially avoided.

E.   Should a "Hostile" LC Filing Be Permitted?

There may be instances when a struggling firm (or its management) believes it can get a better deal in bankruptcy or by holding out for a possible government bail-out. The GSEs, Lehman and AIG all considered these alternatives. All decided to do as the government advised. In the future, other managements might not. The DFA liquidation provisions give the government more formal authority to force a firm into liquidation, but they only apply to large firms that pose a financial stability risk. Moreover, they do not preclude a preemptive bankruptcy filing. This possibility raises the issue of whether a consortium or creditors or other stake holders should be permitted to make a "hostile" liquidity consortium filing (*i.e.*, seek to recapitalize or wind down a struggling firm without the firm management's consent or acquiescence)? Depending on the circumstances, such a filing might be warranted depending on the financial condition of the target and the impact that its failure might have on the stake holders and on the markets. Therefore, the LC model should not preclude formation of an LC where firm management does not consent.

V.   Conclusion

The Financial Crisis of 2007-2008 highlighted certain weaknesses in the regulatory structure with respect to financial firms whose default could have an adverse impact on U.S. market stability. In particular, no adequate means was in place for winding down or recapitalizing such a firm. Congress took an important step toward closing this gap in adopting the orderly liquidation provisions in the Dodd-Frank Act. To accommodate the many political concerns that such a liquidation raises, however, Congress included certain provisions in the Act that have raised legitimate concerns among stakeholders in firms that could be subject to those provisions. While these concerns will lead to improvements in the DFA remains to be seen. What is clear, however, is that the DFA liquidation provisions do not obviate the need for a viable private sector alternative to a government-led liquidation. If anything, uncertainty over how the DFA liquidation provisions will be applied makes the need for a formalized private sector solution all the more pressing. The LTCM crisis illustrated that private liquidity consortia can be an effective means for recapitalizing and winding down struggling firms whose liquidation could adversely impact U.S. financial market stability. The Lehman bankruptcy underscored how an uncertain bankruptcy process can damage market stability and unnecessarily destroy wealth. At this point, it is unclear whether the unpopular DFA liquidation provisions will reduce or increase such uncertainty.

Therefore, a formalized liquidity consortium approach should be considered as an alternative or supplement to the DFA liquidation framework.